Ladies' Home Journal
Easy as 1-2-3
COOKBOOK LIBRARY

Ladies' Home Journal

Easy as 1-2-3

FAMILY FAVORITES
COOKBOOK

by the Editors of Ladies' Home Journal

PUBLISHED BY LADIES' HOME JOURNAL BOOKS

Ladies' Home Journal

Myrna Blyth, Editor-in-Chief
Sue B. Huffman, Food Editor
Jan T. Hazard, Associate Food Editor
Tamara Schneider, Art Director

Produced in association with Media Projects Incorporated

Carter Smith, Executive Editor
Ellen Coffey, Senior Project Editor
Donna Ryan, Project Editor
Bernard Schleifer, Design Consultant
Design by Bruce Glassman

Preface

Most of us remember Mom spending all afternoon cooking. In my household, it seemed that around three-thirty or four, my mother would go into the kitchen and I'd hear the comforting bang of a pot, the slam of the refrigerator door. We ate at six, as soon as my father came home; and though my mother was a good cook and baker, I'm sure we didn't eat an elaborate meal every night. What was my mother doing for nearly three hours? I've never wanted to ask her! But I do know that as I got older and my mother got busier with various activities in her life, she spent less time in the kitchen, and the meals we ate were just as good.

Still, every once in a while I'd love to serve my family one of those homey meals that taste as if they took hours to create. But how can one prepare an old-fashioned favorite in the limited time most of us have for cooking today?

Well, that's a problem we've been discussing and dissecting in Ladies' Home Journal's *test kitchens. We think we've found three ways of handling this gastronomic challenge. In this* Easy as 1-2-3 Family Favorites Cookbook, *you'll find menus full of recipes your family loves, though all the meals can be prepared in thirty minutes or less. How did we do it? By combining new cooking technology, the right ingredients and appropriate cuts of meat, we've created menus that are so substantial, savory and satisfying that you can invite your mom to dinner and even she will think you spent the whole day cooking. (If you tell her the truth, we bet she'll want the recipes!)*

Myrna Blyth
Editor-in-Chief
Ladies' Home Journal

Contents

Chicken Livers in a Creamy Sauce   30
Creamed Chicken Livers, Egg Noodles, Sauteed Broccoli, Quick Key Lime Pie

South-of-the-Border Casserole Menu   36
Tamale Pie, Two-Bean Salad, Tortilla Chips, Mexicali Pudding

Pork Chops Italian Style   40
Pork Pizzaiola, Parmesan Noodles, Stir-Fried or Poached Zucchini, Chocolate Crèmes

Fish Special on the Mealtime Express   42
Baked Fish with Corn Bread Stuffing, Green Beans with Onion Rings, Carrots Julienne with Parsley, Cherry Cheese Tarts

Company-Good Fish Dinner in a Wink   44
Fish Florentine, Rice with Sliced Mushrooms, Pepper Salad, Lemon Tart

Pork and Apples for a Midwinter Warm-Up   46
Normandy Pork Chops, Cottage Potatoes, Green Beans with Sunchokes, Carrot Cake

A Pasta Dinner You Can Whip Up in Minutes   48
Hurry-up Ravioli, Super Salad, Cheesy Herb Rolls, Lemon Sherbet

Stove-Top Casserole with Muffins   50
Spanish Rice, Green Salad with Vinaigrette Dressing, Chilies 'n' Cheese Corn Muffins, Sunrise Sundaes

Satisfying Kielbasa 'n' Sauerkraut   54
Carrot-Orange Soup, Choucroute Garni, Assorted Dark and Light Rolls, Celery and Cucumber Sticks, Pear Upside-Down Ginger Cake

Quick and Colorful Meat Pie   56
Macaroni 'n' Meat Pie, Sauteed Zucchini, Sesame Breadsticks, Mixed Fruit and Cream

Oven-Fried Chicken the Tex-Mex Way   58
El Rancho Chicken, Salsa, Corn with Olives, Green Salad with Avocado and Orange Slices, Cherry Stacks

A Classic Company Dinner   62
Beef Tournedos, Buttered Noodles, Minted Baby Carrots, Green Salad, Mocha Whip

Hearty Pasta Dinner in Minutes   66
Spaghetti with Clam Sauce, Tossed Salad with Creamy Garlic Dressing, Italian Bread, Orange Whip

Corned Beef Hash 'n' Eggs   68
Baked Eggs in Corned Beef Hash Cups, Old-Fashioned Muffins, Fruit Compote

Introduction

Whether you spend all of three hours or just thirty minutes on dinner, you're out of luck if those new recipes you try aren't hits with your family. Now, with the help of our Easy as 1-2-3 Family Favorites Cookbook, *in a mere half hour you can create whole meals that are destined to bring you accolades from your diners, pint-sized to Pop.*

Hurry-Up Ravioli and Sloppy Josés (Sloppy Joes with a Tex-Mex twist) have real appeal for kids. We've all spent hours trying to perfect the ideal Choucroute Garnie. Family Favorites *offers a palate-pleasing version that can be whipped up in thirty minutes flat. The gang will love Normandy Pork Chops flavored with apple cider, and Land's End Chowder will elicit memories of Cape Cod. Country Sausage with Winter Fruit is so mellow you can serve it for Sunday Brunch or for dinner.*

In this complete-menu cookbook, favorite entrees are supplemented with favorite accompaniments—like Carrot-Orange Soup and Chilies 'n' Cheese Corn Muffins. There are Baked Beans Deluxe, Cottage Potatoes, Confetti Rice and a Blue Cheese Dressing that is sensational.

Not to be neglected is the dessert course (after, of course, the kids have consumed their veggies), an honest-to-goodness Dublin Shortbread, an irresistible Pear Upside-Down Ginger Cake, creamy Cherry Cheese Tarts, tempting Candy Store Pudding.

When the troops are starving and time is short, reach for the Easy as 1-2-3 Family Favorites Cookbook.

Sue B. Huffman
Food Editor
Ladies' Home Journal

Chicken Tomato Vinaigrette

COMPANY-PERFECT CHICKEN DINNER

Here are all the elements of a delicious company meal—chicken with a hearty tomato sauce, vegetables dressed up with sauteed almonds and a hot and creamy fruit dessert. Rice-shaped pasta, known as orzo, provides an unusual touch.

Menu for 4

- **Chicken Tomato Vinaigrette Orzo**
- **Broccoli with Sauteed Almonds**
- **Caramel Pears**

SHOPPING LIST

- ☐ 4 chicken cutlets
- ☐ 1 lemon
- ☐ 1 16-ounce can tomatoes
- ☐ 1 bunch fresh basil or dried basil
- ☐ 1 bunch fresh parsley or dried parsley
- ☐ 1 16-ounce package orzo
- ☐ 1 10-ounce package frozen broccoli spears
- ☐ 1 small can or package slivered almonds
- ☐ 1 29-ounce can pear halves
- ☐ ½ pint heavy or whipping cream

Have on Hand
- ☐ Sugar
- ☐ Salt
- ☐ Crushed red pepper
- ☐ Garlic
- ☐ Vanilla extract
- ☐ Wine vinegar
- ☐ Olive oil
- ☐ Butter

SCHEDULE

1. Prepare Caramel Pears.
2. Prepare sauce for Chicken Tomato Vinaigrette.
3. Cook orzo.
4. Cook Chicken Tomato Vinaigrette.
5. Saute almonds; cook broccoli.

Chicken Tomato Vinaigrette

2   tablespoons olive oil, divided
1   garlic clove, crushed
⅛   teaspoon crushed red pepper
1   tablespoon chopped fresh
     basil or ¼ teaspoon dried
1   3-inch strip lemon peel
1   can (16 oz.) tomatoes,
     undrained
½   teaspoon sugar
1   tablespoon wine vinegar
¼   teaspoon salt
2   tablespoons chopped
     parsley, divided
4   chicken cutlets
1   tablespoon butter or
     margarine

In medium stainless steel or enameled saucepan heat 1 tablespoon olive oil over medium heat. Add garlic, red pepper and basil; cook 1 minute. Add lemon peel, tomatoes and sugar, breaking up tomatoes into small chunks. Simmer 20 minutes. Remove from heat; stir in vinegar, salt and 1 tablespoon parsley. Remove lemon peel; set aside.

While sauce cooks, place chicken between 2 sheets of wax paper; pound to ¼- to ½-inch thickness. In large skillet heat remaining tablespoon oil with butter or margarine over medium-high heat. Add chicken. Cook about 3 minutes on each side; remove and keep warm.

Add tomato sauce to skillet; heat 1 minute, stirring constantly. Pour over chicken; sprinkle with remaining parsley.

Caramel Pears

1   can (29 oz.) pear halves,
     drained
3   tablespoons sugar
2   tablespoons butter
½   cup heavy or whipping cream
½   teaspoon vanilla extract

Place broiler rack about 4 inches from heat; preheat broiler. Drain pears on paper towels. Grease 8-inch square baking pan. Arrange pears in pan, cut side down. Sprinkle on sugar evenly; dot with butter. Broil 8 to 10 minutes, rotating pan to brown pears evenly. Remove from broiler.

Reduce oven temperature to 375° F. In small bowl, combine cream and vanilla and pour over pears. Bake 15 minutes until sauce is golden and bubbly.

QUICKEST CHICKENS

What kind of a chicken should you buy when you want to get dinner on the table in a hurry? Here are some hints:

- *Broilers, halved, require about 15 minutes of cooking on each side, 5 inches from heat.*
- *Fryers, cut up, should be cooked 15 to 20 minutes after browning.*
- *Chicken cutlets and boned and skinned chicken breasts cost more per pound than whole chicken, but they need only 3 or 4 minutes of cooking on each side, so they save your valuable time.*

Colcannon with Dinner Sausages

HEARTY AND SATISFYING IRISH COUNTRY SUPPER

On Saint Patrick's Day, on a brisk and windy weekend afternoon or on any cold evening deep in winter, this flavorful meal will be warming and satisfying. To make this an extra-fast treat, pick up a package of shredded cabbage at the supermarket.

═══ Menu for 4 ═══

- **Colcannon with Dinner Sausages**
- **Spiced Peas and Carrots**
- **Dublin Shortbread**

SHOPPING LIST

- ☐ 1 pound smoked sausages
- ☐ 1 pound shredded cabbage
- ☐ 2 bunches green onions
- ☐ 1 small package instant mashed potatoes
- ☐ 1 10-ounce package frozen peas and carrots

Have on Hand

- ☐ All-purpose flour
- ☐ Sugar
- ☐ Cornstarch
- ☐ Salt
- ☐ Pepper
- ☐ Nutmeg
- ☐ Butter
- ☐ Marmalade or strawberry preserves

SCHEDULE

1. Prepare Dublin Shortbread.
2. Prepare Colcannon with Dinner Sausages.
3. Cook Spiced Peas and Carrots.

Colcannon with Dinner Sausages

4 cups shredded cabbage
½ teaspoon salt
1 pound smoked sausages
    Instant mashed potatoes
1 cup sliced green onions,
    divided
1 tablespoon butter or margarine
½ teaspoon pepper

In medium saucepan heat ½ inch water to boiling. Add shredded cabbage and salt. Cover and cook 4 minutes; drain. Meanwhile, in large skillet brown the sausages. Prepare 6 servings instant mashed potatoes according to package directions, adding ¾ cup of the sliced green onions to the liquid. Fold cabbage into potatoes with the butter or margarine and pepper. Spoon onto serving platter; top with sausages and reserved green onions.

Spiced Peas and Carrots

1 package (10 oz.) frozen
    peas and carrots
1 tablespoon butter or margarine
¼ teaspoon salt
⅛ teaspoon nutmeg

In medium saucepan cook peas and carrots according to package directions. Drain; return to saucepan. Add butter or margarine, salt and nutmeg. Cook until heated through.

Dublin Shortbread

1¼ cups all-purpose flour
¼ cup sugar
3 tablespoons cornstarch
½ cup butter, cubed
¼ cup marmalade or
    strawberry preserves

Preheat oven to 375° F. Combine flour, sugar, cornstarch and cubed butter in food processor and blend until finely crumbled, using the on/off method. Press dough evenly into 9-inch spring-form pan with removable bottom. Bake 25 minutes or until golden. Cool 5 minutes; remove rim. Spread marmalade or preserves on top. Cut into 8 wedges.

COOKING TIPS: INSTANT MASHED POTATOES

- *Try instant mashed potatoes right from the package as a no-lump thickener for gravies and white sauces.*
- *Add to stews and casseroles for a richer taste.*
- *Use to create smooth, creamy soups.*
- *For a crisp coating on fried foods, season potato flakes or grains with salt and pepper; roll fish, chicken or vegetables in egg, then potatoes; deep-fry.*

Sloppy Josés

QUICKIE BEEF DINNER WITH A MEXICAN ACCENT

Taco sauce, cheese and chopped chilies turn this sandwich favorite into a new and spicy main dish. Serve the beef mixture over crushed tortilla chips for crunch and flavor. For a tasty and well-balanced year-round dinner, complement the Sloppy Josés with a cool tropical fruit salad. This meal is bound to be popular with the kids (they can even whip it up themselves).

Menu for 4

- **Sloppy Josés Brownies**
- **Grapefruit Avocado Salad**

SHOPPING LIST

- ☐ 1 avocado
- ☐ 1 grapefruit
- ☐ 1 small head leaf lettuce
- ☐ 1 medium and 1 small onion
- ☐ 1 8-ounce bottle or jar taco sauce
- ☐ 1 4-ounce can chopped green chilies
- ☐ 1 package tortilla chips
- ☐ 1 4-ounce package shredded Cheddar cheese
- ☐ 1 pound ground beef
- ☐ Bakery or frozen brownies

Have on Hand
- ☐ Bottled oil and vinegar dressing
- ☐ Cumin
- ☐ Salt

SCHEDULE

1. Prepare Sloppy Josés.
2. Prepare Grapefruit Avocado Salad.

Sloppy Josés

1   pound ground beef
1   medium onion, chopped
1   bottle or jar (8 oz.) taco
    sauce
1   can (4 oz.) chopped green
    chilies
¼   teaspoon salt
2   cups coarsely crushed
    tortilla chips
1   cup shredded Cheddar
    cheese

In large skillet brown beef with onion; pour off drippings. Add taco sauce, chopped chilies and salt. Simmer 8 to 10 minutes. For each serving, spoon mixture over ½ cup crushed tortilla chips and top with ¼ cup grated cheese.

Grapefruit Avocado Salad

1   grapefruit
½   ripe avocado, peeled and
    cubed
1   small onion, sliced
¼   cup bottled oil and vinegar
    dressing
¼   teaspoon ground cumin
    Lettuce leaves

Remove peel and membrane from grapefruit. Slice into thick rings; quarter. In medium bowl combine grapefruit, avocado and onion. In small cup combine oil and vinegar dressing with cumin. Pour over salad; toss. Serve on lettuce leaves.

BUYING AND STORING GRAPEFRUIT

Grapefruit is available in several varieties:
- *Look for grapefruit that is firm and well shaped. It should be fairly smooth and heavy for its size.*
- *White grapefruit is generally tart in taste, and pale yellow inside and out.*
- *Pink grapefruit is sweeter than white, pink inside, and often lightly tinged with pink on the outside.*
- *Ruby red grapefruit is the sweetest of all, colored rosy pink inside, with a ruby blush on the outside.*
- *There's a distinct preference for seedless grapefruit, but don't go into a swivet if you find a seed or two in the so-called seedless fruit you buy. A "seedless" grapefruit is allowed up to 12 seeds—any more and it must drop the seedless claim.*
- *Store grapefruit in the vegetable crisper of your refrigerator or at room temperature if you keep your thermostat below 70 degrees.*

Sauteed Ham Slices

HAM DINNER WITH ALL THE TRIMMINGS

This tasty supper is so easy to prepare that you'll want to show the kids how to do it themselves—it's certain to be one of their favorites. For other hurry-up days, make a note of our handy list of Ham Slice Toppings.

Menu for 4

Sauteed Ham Slices

● **Baked Beans Deluxe**

● **Carrot Slaw Brown Bread**

● **Cherry Crunch**

SHOPPING LIST

- ☐   Ham slices to serve 4
- ☐ 1 small onion
- ☐ 1 bunch green onions
- ☐ 1 pound carrots
- ☐ 2 16-ounce cans pork and beans
- ☐ 1 8¼-ounce can pineapple chunks
- ☐ 1 box natural cereal with raisins and dates
- ☐ 1 21-ounce can cherry pie filling
- ☐   Canned brown bread
- ☐ 1 8-ounce container vanilla yogurt

Have on Hand
- ☐   Bacon

- ☐   Brown sugar
- ☐   Worcestershire sauce
- ☐   Buttermilk dressing
- ☐ 1 lemon or lemon juice
- ☐   Dry mustard
- ☐   Cinnamon
- ☐   Butter or margarine

SCHEDULE

1. Saute ham slices.
2. Prepare Cherry Crunch.
3. Prepare Carrot Slaw.
4. Prepare Baked Beans Deluxe.

Baked Beans Deluxe

2	slices bacon, diced
1	small onion, chopped
2	cans (16 oz. each) pork and beans
2	tablespoons brown sugar
1	tablespoon Worcestershire sauce
1½	teaspoons dry mustard

In medium saucepan cook bacon over medium heat until crisp. To drippings add onion and cook 3 more minutes. Add pork and beans, brown sugar, Worcestershire sauce and mustard. Simmer uncovered over low heat, stirring often, until thickened.

Cherry Crunch

1	can (21 oz.) cherry pie filling
½	teaspoon lemon juice
½	teaspoon cinnamon
1½	cups natural cereal with raisins and dates
2	tablespoons butter or margarine
½	cup vanilla yogurt

Preheat oven to 400° F. In a greased 8-inch square baking dish combine pie filling, lemon juice and cinnamon; sprinkle cereal on top. Dot with butter or margarine. Bake 15 minutes or until bubbly. Serve warm; top with yogurt.

Carrot Slaw

8	medium carrots, shredded
2	green onions, finely chopped
1	can (8¼ oz.) pineapple chunks, drained
¼	cup bottled buttermilk dressing

In medium bowl combine carrots and onions. Stir in pineapple chunks. Add buttermilk dressing and toss.

HAM SLICE TOPPINGS

Always a boon to the hurried cook, ham slices can be baked, sauteed or broiled in a wink. Dress them up with a different topping each time you serve them:

- *Canned pineapple slices*
- *Cherry pie filling*
- *Prepared ham glaze*
- *Brown sugar mixed with cider vinegar*
- *Fruit jelly or preserves thinned with water*

Flounder with Orange Sauce

ELEGANT FISH DINNER FOR FAMILY OR COMPANY

Here's a meal that is beautiful, nourishing and easy to prepare. If you can buy fresh flounder, you'll cut down the cooking time even further. Check often to see if fish flakes easily.

Menu for 4

- **Flounder with Orange Sauce**
- **Anise Rice Broccoli**

- **Watercress and Mushroom Salad Chocolate Eclairs**

SHOPPING LIST

- ☐ 1 head Boston lettuce
- ☐ 1 bunch watercress
- ☐ 8 ounces mushrooms
- ☐ 1 11-ounce can mandarin oranges
- ☐ 1 small jar anise seed
- ☐ 1 13¾- or 14½-ounce can chicken broth
- ☐ 1 10-ounce package frozen broccoli
- ☐ Bakery or frozen chocolate eclairs
- ☐ 1 16-ounce package frozen flounder fillets

Have on Hand
- ☐ Long-grain rice
- ☐ Salt
- ☐ Pepper

- ☐ Garlic
- ☐ Orange juice
- ☐ Butter or margarine
- ☐ Olive oil
- ☐ White wine vinegar
- ☐ Orange marmalade
- ☐ Dijon mustard
- ☐ Dry white wine
- ☐ Brandy

SCHEDULE

1. Prepare Flounder with Orange Sauce.
2. Cook Anise Rice.
3. Cook frozen broccoli.
4. Prepare Watercress and Mushroom Salad.

Flounder with Orange Sauce

1   *package (16 oz.) frozen*
      flounder fillets, partially
      thawed
½   *cup dry white wine*
½   *cup water*
1   *tablespoon butter*
      or margarine
1   *garlic clove, halved*
2   *tablespoons brandy*
½   *cup orange juice*
¼   *cup orange marmalade*
1   *can (11 oz.) mandarin or-*
      ange sections, drained

Preheat oven to 350° F. Cut block of fish diagonally into 4 equal pieces; arrange in 9-inch ovenproof casserole. Pour wine and water over fish. Cover and bake 20 to 25 minutes or until fish flakes easily when tested with a fork.

Meanwhile, in heavy skillet melt butter or margarine over medium heat. Add garlic and saute 1 minute. Add brandy and continue cooking 3 minutes. Add orange juice, marmalade and mandarin orange sections. Pour off poaching liquid from fish and add to orange juice mixture in skillet. Keep fish covered. Increase heat to high and reduce liquid to ¾ cup. Remove from heat. Arrange fish on serving platter; pour sauce over fillets.

Anise Rice

½   *cup long-grain rice*
¼   *teaspoon anise seed*

⅛   *teaspoon salt*
      Chicken broth

Following package directions, cook rice, anise seed and salt in 1-quart saucepan, substituting chicken broth for water.

Watercress and Mushroom Salad

2   *tablespoons olive oil*
1   *tablespoon white wine vinegar*
1   *tablespoon water*
1   *teaspoon Dijon mustard*
¼   *teaspoon salt*
      Generous dash freshly
      ground pepper
6   *cups torn Boston lettuce leaves*
1   *cup watercress sprigs*
1   *cup sliced mushrooms*

In small jar with tight-fitting lid, combine oil, vinegar, water, mustard, salt and pepper. Cover and shake well.

Just before serving, combine lettuce, watercress and mushrooms in salad bowl. Shake dressing and pour over greens. Toss well.

ANISE SEED TIPS

Here are some other ways to use anise seed, which has a delicate licorice-like flavor:

- *Stir into cream cheese or farmers cheese for a tasty spread.*
- *Sprinkle on fresh or thawed frozen fruit.*
- *Sprinkle over cookies or fruit pies before baking.*

Sweet and Sour Pork and Cabbage

BAVARIAN-STYLE PORK FOR WINTER WARMTH

The whole family will enjoy the rich and satisfying flavors of this hearty German meal, which looks and tastes as if it had cooked all day long instead of just thirty minutes. Serve it with traditional accompaniments—noodles, carrots and creamy rice pudding.

=== **Menu for 4** ===

- **Sweet and Sour Pork and Cabbage Egg Noodles**
- **Braised Carrots with Parsley**
- **Jiffy Rice Pudding**

SHOPPING LIST

- ☐ 1 pound pork cube steaks
- ☐ 1 pound carrots
- ☐ 1 medium onion
- ☐ 2 1-pound packages shredded green cabbage
- ☐ 2 cooking apples
- ☐ 1 bunch parsley
- ☐ 1 box enriched precooked rice
- ☐ 1 regular-size package instant vanilla pudding and pie filling
- ☐ 1 13¾- or 14½-ounce can chicken broth

Have on Hand
- ☐ Bacon
- ☐ Egg noodles

- ☐ Brown sugar
- ☐ Salt
- ☐ Cider vinegar
- ☐ Caraway seed
- ☐ Raisins
- ☐ Milk
- ☐ Butter or margarine

SCHEDULE

1. Prepare Sweet and Sour Pork and Cabbage.
2. Prepare Jiffy Rice Pudding; place in freezer to chill.
3. Cook Braised Carrots with Parsley
4. Cook egg noodles.

Sweet and Sour Pork and Cabbage

5   slices bacon, cut into
    ½-inch pieces
1   pound pork cube steaks,
    cut into strips
1   medium onion, chopped
8   cups shredded green
    cabbage
2   cooking apples, cored and
    chopped
⅓   cup cider vinegar
3   tablespoons brown sugar
½   teaspoon salt
¼   teaspoon caraway seed

In Dutch oven cook bacon until crisp; remove and set aside. To drippings add pork and onion and saute for 5 minutes. Stir in remaining ingredients and cook over medium heat for about 25 minutes, stirring occasionally. Transfer with slotted spoon to serving dish; sprinkle with bacon.

Braised Carrots with Parsley

1   pound carrots, peeled and
    halved lengthwise
2   tablespoons butter or
    margarine
2   tablespoons chopped fresh
    parsley
½   cup chicken broth

In large skillet saute carrots in melted butter or margarine over medium heat 5

minutes. Add parsley and broth; cover and cook over low heat 8 to 10 minutes, until carrots are tender.

Jiffy Rice Pudding

1   package (regular size)
    vanilla pudding and
    pie filling
½   cup enriched precooked
    rice
½   cup raisins
2½ cups milk
4   teaspoons brown sugar

In saucepan combine pudding, rice, raisins and milk. Bring to a boil over medium heat and cook until thickened, stirring, 10 to 12 minutes. Spoon into 4 custard cups; sprinkle each with 1 teaspoon brown sugar. Place on cookie sheet; broil until sugar melts, 1 to 2 minutes. Chill.

QUICK SURPRISES WITH RAISINS

Raisins are not only good—and good for you—they're highly versatile:
• *Mix with cream cheese and spread on bread or toast.*
• *Combine with chopped onion and ham to jazz up baked beans.*
• *Add to plain bread stuffing along with equal amounts of chopped apple and pignoli nuts.*

Fried Drumsticks

CRUNCHY FRIED CHICKEN DINNER

Enjoy this chicken dish all winter long, but keep it in mind for next summer's picnics, too. The Blue Cheese Dressing, which is special enough for company meals, can also be prepared with one of the other marbled cheeses mentioned in this menu's Tips.

═══ Menu for 4 ═══

- **Fried Drumsticks**
- **Green Salad with Blue Cheese Dressing**

Potato Puffs
- **Candy Store Pudding**

SHOPPING LIST

- ☐ 8   chicken drumsticks (about 1¾ pounds)
- ☐   Salad greens
- ☐ 1   small onion
- ☐ 1   regular-size package instant chocolate pudding
- ☐ 1   package miniature marshmallows
- ☐ 1   small can or jar cocktail peanuts
- ☐ 2   ounces blue cheese
- ☐ 1   quart buttermilk
- ☐ 1   8-ounce container sour cream
- ☐ ½   pint heavy or whipping cream
- ☐ 1   9-ounce package frozen potato puffs

Have on Hand
- ☐   All-purpose flour

- ☐   Salt
- ☐   Pepper
- ☐   Prepared mustard
- ☐   Onion powder
- ☐   Shortening
- ☐   White vinegar
- ☐   Milk

SCHEDULE

1. Prepare Fried Drumsticks.
2. Heat Frozen Tiny Potato Puffs according to package directions.
3. Prepare Candy Store Pudding; refrigerate.
4. Prepare salad and Blue Cheese Dressing.

Fried Drumsticks

1 cup shortening
8 chicken drumsticks (about
   1¾ lbs.)
⅔ cup buttermilk
¾ cup all-purpose flour
1 teaspoon salt
1 teaspoon onion powder
¼ teaspoon pepper

In large heavy skillet or electric frying pan melt shortening over medium-high heat. Place drumsticks in bowl; pour buttermilk over chicken and turn to coat each piece. Combine dry ingredients in paper or plastic bag; add drumsticks and shake until well coated. Add drumsticks to pan cook until lightly browned, turning frequently. Reduce heat to low, cover and cook 20 minutes, turning occasionally. Remove cover; cook over medium-high heat 3 minutes more to crisp. Drain on paper towels.

Blue Cheese Dressing

1 container (8 oz.) sour
   cream
2 ounces blue cheese,
   crumbled
½ tablespoon white vinegar
½ teaspoon prepared mustard
½ teaspoon grated onion
¼ teaspoon salt

Place all ingredients in blender container. Cover, blend until smooth, stopping blender occasionally and scraping down sides. (Leftover dressing may be refrigated up to 2 days.)

Candy Store Pudding

1 cup heavy or whipping
   cream
1 package (regular size)
   instant chocolate
   pudding
1 cup milk
½ cup miniature
   marshmallows
¼ cup chopped cocktail
   peanuts

In medium bowl whip cream; set aside. In another medium bowl mix chocolate pudding according to package directions, using only 1 cup milk. Fold in cream, marshmallows and chopped peanuts.

THE BLUE CHEESES

Other cheeses in the marbled-blue family—Roquefort, Gorgonzola, Stilton and Danablu—are equally good in a sour cream salad dressing. Properly wrapped, they'll keep in the refrigerator for 3 weeks. Try them also as snacks, crumbled over sour-cream-topped baked potatoes, mixed with cream cheese and cream as a dip, or as dessert with fresh grapes or pears.

Creole Pork Chops

COLORFUL PORK CHOP DINNER

A snappy red sauce, robust with okra and green pep-
pers, provides piquant bite to quickly browned pork
chops. Instead of serving ordinary white rice, make
this meal special by tossing in crumbled bacon,
minced onion and parsley. Prepare dessert in min-
utes; then sit back and enjoy this special dinner.

Menu for 4

- **Creole Pork Chops**
- **Green Salad with Oil and Vinegar Dressing**
- **Confetti Rice Breadsticks**
- **Toffee-Topped Ice Cream Balls**

SHOPPING LIST

- ☐ 8 thin pork chops (about 1½ pounds)
- ☐   Salad greens
- ☐ 1 green pepper
- ☐ 1 medium onion
- ☐ 1 bunch fresh parsley
- ☐ 1 15-ounce can Sloppy Joe sauce
- ☐ 1 13¾- or 14½-ounce can chicken broth
- ☐ 4 1.16-ounce chocolate-coated toffee bars
- ☐ 1 package breadsticks
- ☐ 1 10-ounce package frozen okra
- ☐ 1 pint vanilla ice cream

Have on Hand
- ☐   Bacon
- ☐   Long-grain rice
- ☐   Red pepper sauce
- ☐   Bottled oil and vinegar dressing

SCHEDULE

1. Prepare Confetti Rice.
2. Prepare Creole Pork Chops.
3. Prepare Toffee-Topped Ice Cream Balls.
4. Prepare salad.

Creole Pork Chops

8   thin pork chops
1   package (10 oz.) frozen cut
     okra
1   green pepper, sliced
1   can (15 oz.) Sloppy Joe
     sauce
½   teaspoon red pepper sauce

In large skillet brown pork chops. Thaw okra under hot running water; drain.

Remove chops. To drippings add sliced green pepper and okra. Cook 3 to 4 minutes. Stir in Sloppy Joe sauce and bottled red pepper sauce. Return chops to sauce and simmer, covered, 15 to 20 minutes.

Confetti Rice

1   medium onion, chopped
4   slices bacon, diced
¾   cup long-grain rice
1½   cups chicken broth
       Dash red pepper sauce
2   teaspoons chopped
       parsley

In medium skillet cook onion and bacon over medium heat until bacon pieces are crisp. Add rice, broth and red pepper sauce. Heat to boiling; reduce heat. Cover and simmer 20 minutes. Stir in chopped parsley.

Toffee-Topped Ice Cream Balls

1   pint vanilla ice cream
4   chocolate-coated toffee bars
     (1.16 oz. each), crushed

Use scoop to make 4 ice cream balls; return to freezer. Spread crushed toffee bars in flat dish or pan. Roll ice cream in toffee topping and return to freezer until serving time.

QUICK ZING WITH HOT PEPPER SAUCE

Just a drop or two of pepper sauce will give zest to:
- *packaged corn bread mix*
- *deviled eggs*
- *hollandaise sauce*
- *canned pork and beans*
- *Bloody Marys*
- *ground beef for hamburgers—¼ teaspoon to a pound of beef*
- *shrimp cocktail sauce*
- *omelets, quiches and scrambled eggs*
- *lemon-butter sauces for shrimp or fish fillets*

Lentil Soup with Frankfurters

PROTEIN-PACKED MAIN-DISH SOUP DINNER

You can speed up this quickie meal by letting a food processor do the shredding for you. Nutrient-rich lentils taste wonderful with our tangy cole slaw. These old-fashioned Bran Muffins are delicious plain or dressed up with one of the additions suggested in the Tips section.

Menu for 4

- **Lentil Soup with Frankfurters**
- **Sweet 'n' Sour Cole Slaw**
- **Bran Muffins**

Apple Pie

SHOPPING LIST

- ☐ 2   20-ounce cans ready-to-serve lentil soup
- ☐ 1   16-ounce package frankfurters
- ☐ 1   medium head red cabbage (or packaged shredded cabbage)
- ☐ 1   onion
- ☐ 1   box whole-bran cereal
- ☐ 1   apple pie

Have on Hand
- ☐   Sugar
- ☐   All-purpose flour
- ☐   Baking powder
- ☐   Salt

- ☐   Red pepper sauce
- ☐   White vinegar
- ☐   Salad oil
- ☐   Milk
- ☐   Eggs

SCHEDULE

1. Prepare Bran Muffins.
2. Prepare Sweet 'n' Sour Cole Slaw; refrigerate.
3. Cook Lentil Soup with Frankfurters.

Lentil Soup with Frankfurters

2   cans (20 oz. each) ready-
      to-serve lentil soup
6   frankfurters, cut into
      ½-inch slices
¼   teaspoon red pepper
      sauce

In medium saucepan combine all ingredients. Cover and simmer for 10 minutes, stirring occasionally. Serve hot.

Sweet 'n' Sour Cole Slaw

1   medium head red cabbage,
      finely shredded
⅔   cup white vinegar
½   cup salad oil
⅓   cup sugar
¼   cup chopped onion
½   teaspoon salt

In large bowl combine shredded cabbage with remaining ingredients. Mix well. Cover and chill until serving time. Toss again before serving.

Bran Muffins

1   cup whole-bran cereal
⅔   cup milk
1   cup all-purpose flour
⅓   cup sugar
1   tablespoon baking powder
½   teaspoon salt
¼   cup salad oil
2   eggs, beaten

Preheat oven to 425° F. In small bowl combine cereal and milk. Grease twelve 2½-inch muffin-pan cups; set aside.

In medium bowl combine dry ingredients; mix well. Stir oil and eggs into cereal mixture; add to dry ingredients all at once, stirring just until moistened. Spoon batter into muffin cups, filling each cup ¾ full. Bake about 20 minutes. Immediately remove muffins from pan to wire rack.

BRAN MUFFIN VARIATIONS

To 1 recipe Bran Muffins add (along with the eggs):
- *½ cup each chopped dried apricots and chopped pecans*
- *¾ cup chopped walnuts and ½ cup dark seedless raisins*
- *2 mashed overripe bananas (cool 5 minutes in pan)*
- *½ cup peanut butter-flavored chips*
- *½ cup each shredded carrots and finely chopped dates*

Shrimp Gumbo

SHRIMP DINNER LOUISIANA STYLE

Here is an authentic Louisiana gumbo dinner, complete with okra, rice and corn sticks. Pineapple Foster is a quick and tasty dessert you'll serve often.

Menu for 4

- **Shrimp Gumbo**
Rice
Corn Sticks
- **Green Salad with**
- **Tarragon**
French Dressing
- **Pineapple Foster**

SHOPPING LIST

- ☐ 1½ pounds uncooked shrimp, peeled and deveined
- ☐ 2 onions
- ☐ Salad greens
- ☐ 1 8-ounce can crushed pineapple in juice
- ☐ 1 16-ounce can tomatoes
- ☐ 1 package corn sticks
- ☐ 1 10-ounce package frozen cut okra
- ☐ 1 pint vanilla ice cream

Have on Hand
- ☐ Flour
- ☐ Sugar
- ☐ Dark brown sugar
- ☐ Long-grain rice
- ☐ Salt
- ☐ Pepper

- ☐ Garlic
- ☐ Bay leaves
- ☐ Red pepper sauce
- ☐ Salad oil
- ☐ Tarragon vinegar
- ☐ Dijon-style mustard
- ☐ Butter or margarine
- ☐ Rum

SCHEDULE

1. Prepare Shrimp Gumbo.
2. Cook rice.
3. Prepare salad with Tarragon French Dressing.
4. Prepare Pineapple Foster.

Shrimp Gumbo

4   tablespoons salad oil,
      divided
2   tablespoons flour
1½ pounds uncooked shrimp,
      peeled and deveined
1   package (10 oz.) frozen
      cut okra
2   onions, chopped
1   can (16 oz.) tomatoes,
      undrained
1   quart water
1   bay leaf
3   cloves garlic, crushed
1   teaspoon salt
1   dash red pepper sauce

In small skillet make a *roux* of 2 tablespoons oil and flour. Add shrimp and cook 3 to 5 minutes, stirring constantly. Set aside.

In 4-quart saucepot cook okra and onions in remaining 2 tablespoons oil. Add tomatoes, water, bay leaf, garlic, salt and red pepper sauce. Stir well, then add shrimp and *roux.* Cover and cook slowly 25 minutes.

Tarragon French Dressing

½ cup salad oil
2   tablespoons tarragon vinegar
½ teaspoon salt
⅛ teaspoon pepper
    Dash sugar
¾ teaspoon Dijon-style mustard
1   small garlic clove, minced

In small jar with tight-fitting lid combine oil, tarragon vinegar, salt, pepper, sugar, mustard and garlic; shake well.

Pineapple Foster

2   tablespoons butter or
      margarine
2   tablespoons dark brown
      sugar
1   can (8 oz.) crushed pine-
      apple in juice, undrained
3   tablespoons rum
1   pint vanilla ice cream

In small saucepan melt butter or margarine with brown sugar over moderate heat; stir. Add pineapple with juice and cook for 2 minutes; stir. Add rum; simmer 1 minute longer. Serve over ice cream.

HOW TO PREPARE SHRIMP

- *Shrimp in their shells are usually less expensive than shelled and deveined shrimp. Buy firm shrimp with a slightly sweet odor. One pound in shells equals three servings.*
- *To prepare them for cooking, hold the tail of a shrimp in one hand and a pair of scissors in the other. Slip tip of scissors under shell; snip along center of back. With a gentle tug, pull off shell. Remove black vein. Wash shrimp under cold running water.*

Creamy Chicken Livers

CHICKEN LIVERS IN A CREAMY SAUCE

Cream cheese, condensed soup and vermouth provide a tasty sauce for chicken livers, while sauteed broccoli adds color and crunch to the menu. Our special dessert is as quick as it is delicious; you'll want to serve it the next time guests drop in for dinner.

Menu for 4

- **Creamy Chicken Livers Egg Noodles**
- **Sauteed Broccoli**
- **Quick Key Lime Pie**

SHOPPING LIST

- ☐ 1 pound chicken livers
- ☐ 1 bunch broccoli
- ☐ 3 large or 5 small limes
- ☐ 1 14-ounce can sweetened condensed milk
- ☐ 1 10¾-ounce can condensed creamy chicken mushroom soup
- ☐ 1 9-inch chocolate crumb pie shell
- ☐ 1 3-ounce package cream cheese

Have on Hand
- ☐ Bacon
- ☐ Egg noodles
- ☐ Sugar
- ☐ Salt
- ☐ Pepper

- ☐ Garlic
- ☐ Crushed red pepper
- ☐ Chives
- ☐ Cream of tartar
- ☐ Olive oil
- ☐ Milk
- ☐ Eggs
- ☐ Dry vermouth

SCHEDULE

1. Prepare Quick Key Lime Pie.
2. Cook noodles according to package directions.
3. Prepare Creamy Chicken Livers.
4. Prepare Sauteed Broccoli.

Creamy Chicken Livers

3 strips bacon, cut into
½-inch pieces
1 pound chicken livers, each
cut in half
1 can (10¾ oz.) condensed
creamy chicken mush-
room soup, undiluted
1 package (3 oz.) cream
cheese, cut into pieces
¼ cup milk
¼ cup dry vermouth
2 tablespoons chopped chives
¼ teaspoon pepper

In large skillet over medium heat, cook bacon until crisp; remove from skillet and set aside. To drippings in skillet add chicken livers and cook for 10 minutes, stirring occasionally. With slotted spoon remove livers; set aside. Add remaining ingredients and cook over medium heat, stirring frequently, about 5 minutes. Return bacon and livers to skillet and heat through.

Sauteed Broccoli

2 tablespoons olive oil
1 garlic clove, chopped
¼ teaspoon crushed red pepper
1 bunch broccoli, trimmed
and cut into pieces
½ teaspoon salt

In heavy skillet heat oil; add garlic and crushed red pepper. Add broccoli and turn to coat by shaking pan or tossing broccoli with spoon. Saute over medium heat 7 to 9 minutes or until broccoli is tender but still crisp. Sprinkle with salt.

Quick Key Lime Pie

4 eggs, separated
1 can (14 oz.) sweetened
condensed milk
½ cup fresh lime juice
1 prepared chocolate crumb
pie shell
1 tablespoon sugar
½ teaspoon cream of tartar

Preheat oven to 325° F. In medium bowl beat egg yolks. Add condensed milk and beat until well blended. Slowly add lime juice, mixing well. (Custard will thicken as you add lime juice.) Pour immediately into pie shell. In small mixer bowl beat egg whites until stiff. Add sugar and cream of tartar, beating constantly. Spread meringue over pie filling, covering filling completely and sealing to edges of crust. Bake until delicately browned, 8 to 10 minutes.

MERINGUE TIPS

For perfect meringue every time, keep in mind that eggs should be at room temperature for higher volume. However, separate the eggs while they are still cold; the yolks will be less likely to break. Always use a deep, clean bowl—not plastic—free from grease and soap. Use an electric mixer, and make sure the beaters are also clean and grease free.

Family Favorites Tips

Parsley Tips

Scatter parsley sprigs or chopped parsley over meats or vegetables for a touch of bright greenery. Parsley is clean and delicate in taste, faintly peppery, balanced by a green-apple crispness. The flat-leafed Italian parsley has a stronger flavor.

- *A companion herb, parsley enhances and lends subtlety to stronger herbs. When fresh parsley is combined with dried herbs such as basil or oregano, the result will be a fresh-picked taste.*
- *Fresh bouquets of parsley keep for up to two weeks in the refrigerator if set in a glass of water and covered with a plastic bag.*

Quick and Easy Country Fried Apples

Core and thinly slice 2 pounds cooking apples. In 12-inch skillet melt ¼ cup butter or margarine. Add apples. Saute 10 minutes. In small bowl combine 2 tablespoons sugar with ¼ teaspoon cinnamon; sprinkle over apples. Cook, stirring occasionally, until tender, about 5 minutes more. Makes 4 servings.

Quick Surprises with Raisins

- *Press a couple into each slice of prepared sugar or oatmeal cookie dough, or create patterns with them on the slices to decorate the finished cookie tops.*
- *Stir some into melted currant jelly with a dash of dry mustard for a zesty ham sauce.*
- *Stir some into prepared or deli cole slaw and add crushed pineapple for a sweet variation.*

Fast Sauer-Franks

Brown a sliced onion in butter; add a can of drained sauerkraut, a small can of tomato sauce and two tablespoons brown sugar. Stir together and top with 8 franks. Cover and let simmer about 20 minutes.

Potato Tips

- *Food scientists call potatoes a "nutrient dense" food—which means that per calorie they supply relatively large amounts of vitamins, minerals, proteins and other nutrients. (A food dense in nutrients is the opposite of one that supplies "empty calories.")*
- *A medium-sized raw potato supplies about 35 percent of the minimum daily requirement of vitamin C; 20 percent of vitamin B6; 10 percent of riboflavin; 10 percent of iron; and smaller amounts of most other essential nutrients.*
- *Potatoes have fewer calories than most people realize. A medium baked or boiled potato served "plain" (no butter) has about 100—not many, considering that a cup of unflavored yogurt has 120 calories; ½ cup of cottage cheese has 130; a cup of orange juice has 110; and a three-ounce hamburger patty has 270.*
- *At the market, look for potatoes that are fairly clean, firm, smooth and regular in shape so there will be minimum waste in peeling. For even cooking, select potatoes of uniform size.*
- *When cooking, keep in mind that there are approximately three medium potatoes to the pound, which in turn yields: 3 cups peeled and sliced or 2½ cups peeled and diced or 2 cups mashed or 2 cups french fries.*
- *Better not try to freeze raw or cubed boiled potatoes; they tend to disintegrate when thawed and reheated. If you want to freeze a dish that calls for potato chunks or cubes as an ingredient, make it up without the potatoes, then add them to the dish when reheating. Mashed potatoes shaped into balls or patties, baked stuffed potatoes and french fries can be frozen.*

Tamale Pie, page 36

Tamale Pie

SOUTH-OF-THE-BORDER CASSEROLE MENU

Here is a fast chili main dish with Mexican-style trimmings. This casserole looks as good as it tastes, with its patterned topping of cheese, tortilla chips, olives and shredded lettuce. Round out the meal with an oniony salad of green beans and chick-peas, and end it with a coffee-and-cinnamon-flavored chocolate dessert.

Menu for 4

- **Tamale Pie**
- **Two-Bean Salad**
Tortilla Chips
- **Mexicali Pudding**

SHOPPING LIST

- ☐ 1 small onion
- ☐ 1 head iceberg lettuce
- ☐ 1 8-ounce can creamed corn
- ☐ 1 15-ounce can chili with beans
- ☐ 1 14½-ounce can tamales
- ☐ 1 small can ripe olives
- ☐ 1 small can chick-peas
- ☐ 1 package tortilla chips
- ☐ 1 regular-size package chocolate pudding and pie filling mix
- ☐ 2 4-ounce packages shredded Cheddar cheese
- ☐ 1 9-ounce package frozen cut green beans

Have on Hand
- ☐ Salt
- ☐ Cinnamon
- ☐ Instant coffee
- ☐ Bottled Italian dressing
- ☐ Milk

SCHEDULE

1. Prepare Tamale Pie.
2. Prepare Two-Bean Salad.
3. Prepare Mexicali Pudding.

Tamale Pie

1　can (8 oz.) creamed corn
1　can (15 oz.) chili with
　　beans
1　can (14 ½ oz.) tamales
2　cups shredded Cheddar
　　cheese, divided
¾　cup crushed tortilla chips
　　Shredded lettuce
　　Ripe olives, sliced

Preheat oven to 375° F. In a 2-quart casserole combine creamed corn, chili, tamales and 1 cup shredded Cheddar cheese. Bake 15 minutes. Stir. Sprinkle with crushed tortilla chips, remaining 1 cup shredded Cheddar cheese. Bake 10 minutes. Garnish with shredded lettuce and ripe olives.

Two-Bean Salad

1　package (9 oz.) frozen cut
　　green beans
½　teaspoon salt
1　small onion, sliced
½　cup canned chick-peas,
　　drained
2　tablespoons bottled Italian
　　dressing

In saucepan cook frozen green beans in ½ inch boiling water with ½ teaspoon salt 6 minutes. Drain; chill with cold water. Drain again. In medium bowl combine beans with sliced onion and chick-peas. Toss with Italian dressing. Refrigerate until serving time.

Mexicali Pudding

1　package (regular size)
　　chocolate pudding and
　　pie filling mix
1　tablespoon instant coffee
　　granules
⅛　teaspoon cinnamon
2　cups milk

In medium saucepan combine pudding mix, instant coffee and cinnamon. Slowly stir in milk. Bring to a full boil over medium heat, stirring constantly. Pour pudding into 4 serving dishes; cover and chill in freezer until serving time.

START WITH A PACKAGE OF FROZEN GREEN BEANS . . .

Prepare frozen green beans according to package directions and:

- *Combine with crumbled fried bacon, cooked diced onion and a dash of red pepper sauce.*
- *Chill and toss with sour cream, sliced cucumber and a pinch of dill.*
- *Combine with sauteed onion and a teaspoon of curry powder as a complement to lamb or fish.*
- *Add to omelets along with some grated cheese; cook until set and sprinkle with more cheese; run under broiler.*

Pork Pizziola, page 40

Baked Fish with Corn Bread Stuffing, page 42

Fish Florentine, page 44

Normandy Pork Chops, page 46

Hurry-Up Ravioli, page 48

Assorted Muffins, page 50

Pork Pizzaiola

PORK CHOPS ITALIAN STYLE

Thick and juicy loin pork chops—or twice as many quick-cooking skinny ones, if you're in a special hurry—simmer in a thick tomato sauce while you whip up the rest of the meal. This delightful Italian menu, with a light but luscious dessert, will win raves from the dinner-table critics.

Menu for 4

- **Pork Pizzaiola**
- **Parmesan Noodles**
- **Stir-Fried or Poached Zucchini**
- **Chocolate Crèmes**

SHOPPING LIST

- ☐ 4   pork loin chops
- ☐ 1   green pepper
- ☐ 1   onion
- ☐ 3   medium zucchini
- ☐ 1   bunch fresh parsley or dried parsley
- ☐ 1   16-ounce jar Italian-style cooking sauce
- ☐ 1   6-ounce package semisweet chocolate chips
- ☐ 1   pint half and half cream
- ☐ ½   pint heavy or whipping cream

Have on Hand

- ☐   Salt
- ☐   Pepper
- ☐   Egg noodles
- ☐   Salad oil
- ☐   Butter
- ☐   Grated Parmesan cheese
- ☐   Eggs
- ☐   Milk
- ☐   Rum

SCHEDULE

1. Prepare Chocolate Crèmes.
2. Prepare Pork Pizzaiola; cover and simmer.
3. Cook noodles.
4. Prepare and cook zucchini.

Pork Pizzaiola

1 tablespoon salad oil
4 pork loin chops
1 green pepper, thinly sliced
1 onion, thinly sliced
2 cups Italian-style cooking
    sauce

In large skillet heat oil. Brown chops on both sides; drain off all but 1 tablespoon fat. Add pepper and onion to skillet. Saute 3 to 5 minutes. Stir in Italian-style sauce. Cover and simmer 15 to 20 minutes or until chops are cooked through.

Parmesan Noodles

3 cups medium egg noodles
1/4 cup half and half cream
1 tablespoon butter or
    margarine
1/2 cup grated Parmesan
    cheese
1 tablespoon chopped parsley
1/4 teaspoon freshly ground
    pepper

Cook noodles according to package directions; drain. Heat cream with butter or margarine. Toss with noodles. Add grated Parmesan, parsley and pepper. Toss again.

Chocolate Crèmes

1 egg
1/2 cup semisweet chocolate
    chips
1/4 cup milk, scalded
1 tablespoon rum
1/2 cup heavy cream

Whip egg in blender container 5 seconds. Add chocolate chips and scalded milk; blend until smooth. Add rum and blend 5 more seconds. Transfer to bowl; place in freezer, stirring often, until cool, about 15 minutes.

Whip heavy cream until stiff. Fold into chocolate mixture. Pour into parfait glasses; refrigerate until serving time.

BUYING THE RIGHT SIZED PORK CHOPS

Look for pork chops cut on the thin side. Skinny chops need only about 7 minutes of cooking time on each side, or a total of 14 minutes as opposed to the usual 30 to 40 minutes. Instead of serving one thick chop for each person, you can offer two thinner ones cooked in half the time.

Baked Fish with Corn Bread Stuffing

FISH SPECIAL ON THE MEALTIME EXPRESS

Save this tempting fall or winter menu for days when you're racing to meet the dinner deadline. All but the carrot julienne is assembled with convenience foods you'll find at hand on your shelves or in your freezer.

Menu for 4

- **Baked Fish with Corn Bread Stuffing**
  Green Beans with Onion Rings
- **Carrots Julienne with Parsley**
- **Cherry Cheese Tarts**

SHOPPING LIST

- ☐ 1   onion
- ☐ 1   bunch celery
- ☐ 1   bunch fresh parsley
- ☐ 2   lemons òr 1 lemon and lemon juice
- ☐ 1   6-ounce package corn bread stuffing mix
- ☐ 1   16-ounce can green beans
- ☐ 4   graham cracker tart shells
- ☐ 1   21-ounce can cherry pie filling
- ☐ 1   can fried onion rings
- ☐ 1   8-ounce package cream cheese
- ☐ 1   16-ounce package frozen fish fillets

Have on Hand
- ☐   Sugar
- ☐   Salt
- ☐   Pepper
- ☐   Paprika
- ☐   Vanilla extract
- ☐   Mayonnaise
- ☐   Butter or margarine
- ☐   Eggs

SCHEDULE

1. Prepare Baked Fish with Corn Bread Stuffing.
2. Make Cherry Cheese Tarts; refrigerate.
3. Prepare Green Beans.
4. Prepare Carrots.

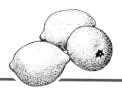

Baked Fish with Corn Bread Stuffing

1   package (16 oz.) frozen
     fish fillets, thawed 10
     minutes
1   tablespoon butter or
     margarine
1   small onion, chopped
1   celery rib, chopped
1½   cups water
1   package (6 oz.) corn
     bread stuffing mix
¼   cup plus 2 teaspoons
     mayonnaise
2   teaspoons lemon juice
¼   teaspoon salt
⅛   teaspoon pepper
     Paprika
     Lemon wedges
     Parsley

Preheat oven to 375° F. Cut partially thawed fish into 4 portions. In medium saucepan melt butter or margarine. Add onion and celery and saute. Add water and contents of vegetable seasoning packet from stuffing mix package. Bring to a boil. Reduce heat, cover and simmer 5 minutes. Stir in stuffing mix. Tightly cover; let stand 5 minutes. Then stir in ¼ cup mayonnaise.

Spoon dressing into individual oven-proof dishes or shallow 1-quart casserole. Top with fish; spread ½ teaspoon mayonnaise on each piece. Sprinkle with lemon juice, salt, dash each pepper and paprika. Cover with foil. Bake 20 minutes or until fish flakes easily. Remove foil; bake 2 to 3 minutes more, until mayonnaise is lightly browned. Garnish with lemon wedges and parsley.

Cherry Cheese Tarts

1   package (8 oz.) cream
     cheese, softened
1   egg yolk
2   tablespoons sugar
2   teaspoons vanilla extract
1   tablespoon lemon juice
4   packaged graham cracker
     tart shells
¼   cup canned cherry pie
     filling.

In small mixer bowl, beat cream cheese, egg yolk, sugar, vanilla and lemon juice until smooth. Spoon into tart shells. Top each with 1 tablespoon pie filling. Refrigerate until serving time.

TART SHELL TIPS

Fill prepared graham cracker tart shells with:
- *sliced canned peaches glazed with melted peach preserves and topped with shredded coconut*
- *dairy-case chocolate pudding with a dollop of whipped cream*
- *sliced bananas topped with instant vanilla pudding*

Fish Florentine

COMPANY-GOOD FISH DINNER IN A WINK

Here's a tasty fish entree in the Florentine style made from wholesome frozen foods. This salad and dessert are so easy and delicious that you will want to add them to your list of favorites. And when you're in a real rush, try our super-quick frozen fish Tips.

Menu for 4

- **Fish Florentine**
  Rice with Sliced
  Mushrooms
- **Pepper Salad**
- **Lemon Tarts**

SHOPPING LIST

- ☐ 2 small onions
- ☐ 2 red or green peppers
- ☐ 1 head lettuce
- ☐ 2 lemons
- ☐ 1 14-ounce can sweetened condensed milk
- ☐ 1 11-ounce can condensed Cheddar cheese soup
- ☐ 6 prepared individual graham cracker tart shells
- ☐ 1 12-ounce package frozen breaded fish portions
- ☐ 1 10-ounce package frozen chopped spinach

Have on Hand
- ☐ Sugar
- ☐ Salt
- ☐ Pepper
- ☐ Worcestershire sauce

- ☐ Red wine vinegar
- ☐ Salad oil
- ☐ Butter or margarine
- ☐ Eggs
- ☐ Milk
- ☐ Vermouth

SCHEDULE

1. Prepare Lemon Tarts.
2. Cook rice; slice and briefly saute mushrooms.
3. Bake frozen fish; cook frozen spinach.
4. Prepare Pepper Salad.
5. Prepare Fish Florentine.
6. Toss together rice and mushrooms.

Fish Florentine

1	package (12 oz.) breaded fish portions
1	package (10 oz.) frozen chopped spinach
2	tablespoons butter or margarine
1/4	cup chopped onion
1	can (11 oz.) condensed Cheddar cheese soup, undiluted
1/3	cup milk
2	tablespoons vermouth
1 1/2	teaspoons Worcestershire sauce

Bake frozen fish portions and cook spinach according to package directions (omit salt). In small saucepan melt butter or margarine. Add chopped onion and saute until tender. Add condensed Cheddar cheese soup, milk, vermouth and Worcestershire sauce. Heat to boiling, stirring frequently. Reduce heat and simmer 3 minutes. To serve, stir ⅔ cup cheese sauce into drained spinach and spoon into a serving dish. Top with fish and spoon on remaining sauce.

Pepper Salad

2	tablespoons red wine vinegar
2	tablespoons salad oil
2	tablespoons water
1/8	teaspoon salt
	Dash pepper
	Dash sugar
2	red or green peppers, julienned
1	small onion, sliced
	Lettuce

In jar with tight-fitting lid combine vinegar, salad oil, water, salt, pepper and sugar. Cover and shake until well mixed. In medium bowl combine pepper strips and sliced onion. Pour over dressing and toss. Serve on lettuce-lined salad plates.

Lemon Tarts

1	can (14 oz.) sweetened condensed milk
2	eggs
1/2	cup lemon juice
1	teaspoon grated lemon peel
6	prepared individual graham cracker tart shells

In medium bowl combine condensed milk, eggs, lemon juice and grated lemon peel; stir until well blended. Pour into tart shells. Refrigerate until ready to serve.

QUICK TRICKS WITH FROZEN FISH PORTIONS

Here are two super-fast entrees that start with a package of frozen breaded fish portions:

- *Deviled Fish. Combine 1/4 cup barbecue sauce with 1 teaspoon prepared mustard and 1 cup diced processed cheese. Spread over fish portions. Bake at 375° F. 20 to 25 minutes.*
- *Fish in a Pocket. Serve prepared fish portions in pita bread with prepared cole slaw.*

Normandy Pork Chops

PORK AND APPLES FOR A MIDWINTER WARM-UP

Try this quick and interesting twist on the classic pork-and-apples combination and round out the meal with double-cheese-rich potatoes. Sunchokes (Jerusalem artichokes) may be a new name on your shopping list. You'll like their crunchy texture.

Menu for 4

- **Normandy Pork Chops**
- **Cottage Potatoes**
- **Green Beans with Sunchokes**
  Carrot Cake

SHOPPING LIST

- ☐ 8 thin pork chops
- ☐ 2 apples
- ☐ 1 bunch fresh parsley
- ☐ 2 sunchokes or one 11-ounce can water chestnuts
- ☐ 1 8-ounce container creamed cottage cheese
- ☐ 1 4-ounce package shredded Cheddar cheese
- ☐ 1 9-ounce package frozen French-style green beans
- ☐ 1 package frozen chopped onion
- ☐ 1 carrot cake
- ☐ Apple cider or juice

Have on Hand
- ☐ Cornstarch
- ☐ Salt
- ☐ Pepper
- ☐ Marjoram
- ☐ Chives
- ☐ Salad oil
- ☐ Butter or margarine
- ☐ Instant mashed potatoes

SCHEDULE

1. Prepare Cottage Potatoes.
2. Prepare Normandy Pork Chops.
3. Prepare Green Beans with Sunchokes.

Normandy Pork Chops

1   *tablespoon salad oil*
8   *thin pork chops*
½ *cup frozen chopped onion*
¾ *teaspoon salt*
1   *cup apple cider or juice,*
     divided
2   *unpeeled apples, cored and*
     cut into wedges
1   *tablespoon cornstarch*
     Chopped parsley

In large skillet heat salad oil. Brown pork chops; remove. Add onion; saute 2 minutes. Return chops to skillet and sprinkle with salt. Add ¾ cup cider or juice. Top with apple wedges. Cover and simmer 15 minutes.

Dissolve cornstarch in remaining ¼ cup cider. Transfer chops and apples to serving dish. Stir cornstarch mixture into skillet. Bring to a boil; cook 1 minute, stirring. Pour sauce over chops. Sprinkle with chopped parsley.

Cottage Potatoes

     Instant mashed potatoes
¾ *cup creamed cottage cheese*
1   *cup shredded Cheddar*
     cheese
1   *tablespoon chopped chives*
     Dash freshly ground
     pepper
1   *tablespoon butter or*
     margarine

Preheat oven to 375° F. In medium bowl prepare instant mashed potatoes according to package directions for 6 servings, *omitting milk and salt*. Fold in creamed cottage cheese, shredded Cheddar cheese, chopped chives and pepper. Spoon into greased casserole and dot with butter or margarine. Bake 25 minutes.

Green Beans with Sunchokes

1   *package (9 oz.) frozen*
     French-style green beans
1   *tablespoon butter or margarine*
¼ *teaspoon salt*
     Dash pepper
½ *teaspoon marjoram*
½ *cup unpeeled julienned*
     sunchokes or ½ cup
     water chestnuts

In medium saucepan cook green beans according to package directions; drain. Add butter or margarine, salt, pepper, marjoram and sunchokes or water chestnuts. Toss well and cook until heated through.

GREEN BEAN MAGIC

What can you add to green beans besides the exotic sunchoke? Almost anything! Top them with:
- *chopped cashews sauteed in butter*
- *canned fried onion rings*
- *grated orange or lemon peel*
- *prepared French dressing*
- *crispy crumbled bacon*

Hurry-up Ravioli

A PASTA DINNER YOU CAN WHIP UP IN MINUTES

A creamy sauce, rich with bits of ham, tops off this variation on a favorite Italian specialty—ravioli. The theme is echoed in Parmesan-accented rolls and a tangy salad of Mediterranean vegetables.

================= **Menu for 4** =================

- **Hurry-Up Ravioli**
- **Super Salad**

- **Cheesy Herb Rolls**

  Fresh Cherries

SHOPPING LIST

- ☐ 1 13¾- or 14½-ounce can chicken broth
- ☐ 1 4-ounce jar roasted red peppers
- ☐ 1 6-ounce jar marinated artichoke hearts
- ☐ Fresh cherries
- ☐ 1 small head romaine lettuce
- ☐ 1 package brown-and-serve rolls
- ☐ 1 10-ounce package frozen green peas
- ☐ ½ pound cooked ham in ½-inch slices
- ☐ 1 pound fresh or frozen cheese ravioli

Have on Hand
- ☐ Sugar
- ☐ All-purpose flour
- ☐ Pepper
- ☐ Milk
- ☐ Butter or margarine
- ☐ Grated Parmesan cheese
- ☐ White wine vinegar
- ☐ Salad oil
- ☐ Garlic
- ☐ Oregano

SCHEDULE

1. Prepare salad and dressing.
2. Cook ravioli according to package directions.
3. Prepare Cheesy Herb Rolls.
4. Cook sauce; assemble Hurry-Up Ravioli.

Hurry-Up Ravioli

3   *tablespoons butter or*
      margarine
¼   *cup flour*
1½ *cups milk*
½   *cup chicken broth*
⅛   *teaspoon pepper*
1   *cup frozen green peas*
½   *cup grated Parmesan*
      cheese
1   *cup julienned ham*
1   *pound fresh or frozen*
      cheese ravioli

In medium saucepan melt butter or margarine over medium heat. Whisk in flour; cook 1 minute. Slowly add milk and chicken broth; cook, stirring, until thickened. Add pepper and peas. Gradually add grated Parmesan cheese, stirring until melted. Mix in julienned ham.

Meanwhile, cook ravioli according to package directions. Drain well. Toss with sauce; spoon onto serving platter.

Super Salad

1   *jar (6 oz.) marinated*
      artichoke hearts
1   *small head romaine*
      lettuce, torn into pieces
2   *tablespoons roasted red*
      peppers, julienned
1½ *tablespoons white wine*
      vinegar
1   *tablespoon salad oil*
¼   *teaspoon freshly ground*
      pepper
¼   *teaspoon sugar*

1   *small garlic clove,*
      crushed

Drain artichokes, reserving the marinade. In a salad bowl combine artichokes, romaine and julienned red peppers. In jar with tight-fitting lid combine reserved marinade, vinegar, oil, pepper, sugar and garlic. Cover and shake well. Pour over salad, toss well and serve.

Cheesy Herb Rolls

4   *brown-and-serve rolls*
      Butter
1   *tablespoon grated*
      Parmesan cheese
¼   *teaspoon oregano*

Preheat oven to 350° F. Cut rolls in half; butter the cut sides. Sprinkle evenly with grated cheese and oregano. Bake on cookie sheet 10 minutes or until rolls are lightly browned.

PDQ Pasta

Here's another fast and easy pasta entree. Serve it with garlic bread and a tossed salad. Prepare according to package directions 2 packages (11 oz. each) frozen creamed chipped beef, 1 package (10 oz.) frozen peas with pearl onions and ½ pound thin spaghetti. In large serving bowl combine all ingredients and add a dash of Worcestershire sauce.

Spanish Rice

STOVE-TOP CASSEROLE WITH MUFFINS

Spicy pork sausage, chopped green pepper and chilies give distinctive flavor to this version of Spanish Rice. Pop the muffins in the oven to bake while you prepare the main dish.

═══ Menu for 4 ═══

- **Spanish Rice**
  Green Salad with
  Vinaigrette
  Dressing
- **Chilies 'n'**
  Cheese Corn
  Muffins
- **Sunrise Sundaes**

SHOPPING LIST

- ☐ 1   12-ounce package bulk pork sausage
- ☐ 1   green pepper
- ☐   Salad greens
- ☐ 1   1½-ounce envelope Mexican rice seasoning mix
- ☐ 1   16-ounce can stewed tomatoes
- ☐ 2   4-ounce cans chopped green chilies
- ☐ 1   4-ounce package shredded Cheddar cheese
- ☐ 1   10-ounce package frozen green peas
- ☐ 1   pint orange sherbet
- ☐   Tequila
- ☐   Grenadine

Have on Hand
- ☐   Long-grain rice

- ☐   All-purpose flour
- ☐   Yellow cornmeal
- ☐   Sugar
- ☐   Baking powder
- ☐   Salt
- ☐   Pepper
- ☐   Salad oil
- ☐   Vinegar
- ☐   Milk
- ☐   Eggs

SCHEDULE

1. Preheat oven; prepare Chilies 'n' Cheese Muffins.
2. Prepare Spanish Rice.
3. Toss salad.
4. Prepare Sunrise Sundaes.

Spanish Rice

1   package (12 oz.) bulk pork
      sausage, broken into chunks
1/2   cup chopped green pepper
1   cup long-grain rice
1   envelope (1 1/2 oz.) Mexican
      rice seasoning mix
1   can (16 oz.) stewed tomatoes
2   cups water
2   tablespoons canned
      chopped green chilies
1   package (10 oz.) frozen
      green peas

In large skillet over medium-high heat, cook sausage 5 minutes, stirring occasionally. Spoon off all but 2 tablespoons drippings. Add green pepper and rice and saute, stirring occasionally, 2 minutes. Add remaining ingredients except peas. Heat to boiling. Reduce heat; cover and simmer 15 minutes. Add peas and cook 5 more minutes.

Chilies 'n' Cheese Corn Muffins

1   cup all-purpose flour
3/4   cup yellow cornmeal
3   tablespoons sugar
4   teaspoons baking powder
1/2   teaspoon salt
1   cup shredded Cheddar cheese
1   can (4 oz.) chopped green
      chilies, well drained
1   cup milk
1/4   cup salad oil
2   eggs, beaten

Preheat oven to 425° F. Grease twelve 2 1/2-inch muffin-pan cups; set aside. In medium bowl combine dry ingredients; mix well. Mix in Cheddar and chilies. In 2-cup measure combine milk, oil and eggs. Add to dry ingredients all at once. Stir just until moistened. Spoon batter into muffin pan, filling each cup 3/4 full. Bake about 20 minutes. Immediately remove muffins from pan to wire rack.

Sunrise Sundaes

1   pint orange sherbet
1/2   cup tequila
1/2   cup grenadine

Place 1 scoop sherbet in each of 4 dessert dishes or parfait glasses. Pour 2 tablespoons tequila and 1 tablespoon grenadine over each.

CORN MUFFIN VARIATIONS

After you stir in the liquid, try adding the following in place of chilies and cheese:
- *1 1/2 cups blueberries (cool muffins in pan 5 minutes)*
- *2 tablespoons dark molasses*
- *1/4 cup minced green pepper, 1/2 cup whole-kernel corn and 1/4 teaspoon crushed red pepper*
- *1 cup finely chopped Swiss cheese and 1/2 cup finely chopped cooked ham or salami*

Choucroute Garni, page 54

Macaroni and Meat Pie, page 56

El Rancho Chicken, page 58 ♦

Choucroute Garni

SATISFYING KIELBASA 'N' SAUERKRAUT

While you enjoy the quick blender soup, the Choucroute Garni will cook to a turn. You'll want to offer the upside-down cake warm from the oven.

Menu for 4

- **Carrot-Orange Soup**
- **Choucroute Garni Assorted Dark and Light Rolls**
- **Celery and Cucumber Sticks**
- **Pear Upside-Down Ginger Cake**

SHOPPING LIST

- ☐ 1 pound Polish sausage (kielbasa)
- ☐ 2 medium onions
- ☐ 1 small potato
- ☐ 1 bunch celery
- ☐ 1 cucumber
- ☐ 1 pound sauerkraut
- ☐ 1 13¾- or 14½-ounce can chicken broth
- ☐ 1 8-ounce jar applesauce
- ☐ 1 16-ounce can carrots
- ☐ 1 6-ounce can orange juice concentrate
- ☐ 1 16-ounce can pear halves
- ☐ 1 14-ounce package gingerbread mix
- ☐   Dark and light rolls
- ☐ ½ pint heavy or whipping cream

Have on Hand
- ☐   Bacon
- ☐   Brown sugar
- ☐   Nutmeg
- ☐   Caraway seed
- ☐   Butter or margarine

SCHEDULE

1. Prepare Choucroute Garni.
2. Mix and bake Pear Upside-Down Ginger Cake.
3. Prepare Carrot-Orange Soup.

Carrot-Orange Soup

1   tablespoon butter or
       margarine
1   medium onion, chopped
1   can (16 oz.) carrots,
       undrained
¾   cup chicken broth
2   tablespoons undiluted
       orange juice
       concentrate
½   teaspoon nutmeg

In medium saucepan melt butter or margarine. Add chopped onion and saute until translucent. Spoon into blender container. Add undrained carrots, chicken broth, orange juice concentrate and nutmeg. Blend until smooth. Cook over low heat 5 minutes.

Choucroute Garni

1   pound Polish sausage
       (kielbasa)
4   slices bacon, diced
1   medium onion, chopped
1   small potato, grated
3   cups sauerkraut, rinsed
       and drained
1   cup chicken broth
⅔   cup applesauce
1   tablespoon brown sugar
½   teaspoon caraway seed

Score Polish sausage at 1-inch intervals; set aside. In large skillet brown bacon. Add onion and potato to drippings. Cook until tender. Add sauerkraut, chicken broth, applesauce, brown sugar and caraway seed. Stir; add sausage. Cover and simmer 25 minutes.

Pear Upside-Down Ginger Cake

3   tablespoons butter or
       margarine
½   cup firmly packed light
       brown sugar
1   can (16 oz.) pear halves,
       drained
1   package (14 oz.) ginger-
       bread mix
       Whipped cream (optional)

Preheat oven to 375° F. In a 9-inch square baking pan melt butter or margarine in oven. Remove from oven; stir in brown sugar. Arrange drained pear halves in pan over brown sugar syrup. Prepare gingerbread mix according to package directions. Pour batter over pears. Bake 30 minutes or until toothpick inserted in center comes out clean. Cool in pan 2 minutes. Invert onto plate. Top with whipped cream, if desired.

START WITH A CAN OF FROZEN ORANGE JUICE . . .

Orange Chicken—*Dilute concentrate with 1 cup water; add rosemary and pour over browned cut-up chicken. Bake 1 hour in 350° F. oven; top with sliced almonds.*

Macaroni 'n' Meat Pie

QUICK AND COLORFUL MEAT PIE

The crust of this hearty pie is a savory meatloaf blend, the filling macaroni and cheese. Round out this dinner with Italian-style zucchini, crunchy bread sticks and a smooth and luscious fruit-and-cream dessert.

Menu for 4

- **Macaroni 'n' Meat Pie**
- **Sauteed Zucchini**
- **Sesame Breadsticks**
- **Mixed Fruit and Cream**

SHOPPING LIST

- ☐ 1 7-ounce package macaroni and cheese
- ☐ 1 small onion
- ☐ 1 tomato
- ☐ 1 pound zucchini (about 3 medium)
- ☐ 2 bananas
- ☐ 1 17-ounce jar refrigerated fruit salad
- ☐ 1 small can or package sliced almonds
- ☐ 1 8-ounce container sour cream
- ☐ 1 pound ground beef

Have on Hand
- ☐ Brown sugar
- ☐ Uncooked oats
- ☐ Salt
- ☐ Pepper
- ☐ Italian herb seasoning or basil
- ☐ Salad oil
- ☐ Ketchup
- ☐ Worcestershire sauce
- ☐ Eggs
- ☐ Parmesan cheese

SCHEDULE

1. Prepare Macaroni 'n' Meat Pie.
2. Cook Sauteed Zucchini.
3. Prepare Mixed Fruit and Cream.

Macaroni 'n' Meat Pie

1   pound ground beef
¼   cup ketchup
¼   cup uncooked oats
2   tablespoons water
1   tablespoon Worcestershire
        sauce
1   small onion, chopped
1   teaspoon salt
2   eggs
1   package (7 oz.) macaroni
        and cheese
¼   cup grated Parmesan cheese
1   tomato

Preheat oven to 400° F. In medium bowl mix ground beef, ketchup, oats, water and Worcestershire sauce. Stir in chopped onion and salt. Beat 1 egg and add to meat mixture. Pat into 9-inch pie plate; bake 10 minutes.

Meanwhile, prepare macaroni and cheese according to package directions. Beat remaining egg and add to macaroni and cheese. Remove pie plate from oven and carefully drain off excess fat. Spoon macaroni into meat shell and sprinkle on grated Parmesan cheese. Cut tomato into wedges and arrange on top of casserole. Return to oven and bake 10 minutes more. Cut into wedges.

Sauteed Zucchini

1   tablespoon salad oil
3   medium zucchini (about
        1 pound), sliced
¼   teaspoon Italian herb
        seasoning or basil
¼   teaspoon salt
        Dash pepper
1   tablespoon water

In a large skillet heat oil. Add zucchini, herb seasoning or basil, salt and pepper. Stir until zucchini is well coated. Add water; cover and simmer 5 minutes or until zucchini is tender.

Mixed Fruit and Cream

1   jar (17 oz.) refrigerated
        fruit salad, drained
2   bananas, sliced
½   cup sour cream
1   tablespoon brown sugar
2   tablespoons sliced almonds

In medium bowl combine fruit salad and bananas; toss gently. Divide fruit among 4 dessert bowls. In 1-cup measure combine sour cream and brown sugar; spoon over fruit. Sprinkle with sliced almonds.

SOUR CREAM DIP TIP

For a tangy Mexican accent combine 1 cup sour cream, 1 can (10½ oz.) jalapeño bean dip, ¼ cup chopped onion, ¼ teaspoon bottled red pepper sauce and 1 teaspoon Worcestershire sauce. Stir until blended.

El Rancho Chicken

OVEN-FRIED CHICKEN THE TEX-MEX WAY

Accompanied by a medley of corn and diced red or green pepper, this quick oven chicken is sure to become a standard company meal.

Menu for 6

- **El Rancho Chicken Salsa**
- **Corn with Olives**

Green Salad with Avocado and Orange Slices
- **Cherry Stacks**

SHOPPING LIST

- ☐ 6 chicken cutlets
- ☐ 1 red or green pepper
- ☐ 1 medium onion
- ☐ 1 bunch parsley
- ☐ Salad greens
- ☐ 2 large oranges
- ☐ 1 avocado
- ☐ 1 small bottle or jar salsa
- ☐ 1 7½-ounce package nacho or tortilla chips
- ☐ 1 small can ripe olives
- ☐ 1 21-ounce can cherry pie filling
- ☐ 1 17-ounce roll slice 'n' bake refrigerated sugar cookies
- ☐ 1 bottle or jar refrigerated buttermilk spice salad dressing

- ☐ 1 8-ounce container frozen whipped topping with real cream
- ☐ 2 10-ounce packages frozen whole kernel corn

Have on Hand
- ☐ Salt
- ☐ Pepper
- ☐ Butter or margarine
- ☐ Amaretto or kirsch (optional)

SCHEDULE

1. Prepare Cherry Stacks.
2. Prepare and bake El Rancho Chicken.
3. Make salad.
4. Prepare Corn with Olives.

El Rancho Chicken

6   chicken cutlets
¾   cup refrigerated butter-
      milk spice salad
      dressing
2⅓ cups (about 6 oz.) crushed
      nacho cheese chips or
      tortilla chips

Preheat oven to 350° F. Grease a large cookie sheet. Pound chicken breasts between 2 sheets wax paper. Spoon dressing into large shallow bowl and crushed chips into second bowl. Dip chicken into salad dressing to coat, then in crushed chips. Place on cookie sheet. Bake 25 minutes.

Corn with Olives

2   packages (10 oz. each)
      frozen whole kernel
      corn
¼   cup butter or margarine
1   medium onion, chopped
1   red or green pepper, diced
¼   cup sliced ripe olives
¼   teaspoon salt
      Dash pepper
¼   cup minced fresh parsley

Cook corn according to package directions; drain well. In a large skillet melt butter or margarine and saute onion and green pepper 5 minutes. Add corn, olives, salt and pepper. Stir in parsley.

Cherry Stacks

¾   of a 17-oz. roll slice 'n' bake
      refrigerated sugar cookies
1   can (21 oz.) cherry pie filling
1   tablespoon amaretto or
      kirsch (optional)
1   cup frozen whipped topping
      with real cream, thawed

Preheat oven to 375° F. Slice cookie dough ⅛ inch thick into 36 slices. Arrange 3 slices on ungreased cookie sheet in an overlapping circle. Repeat to form 12 large cookies, using 2 cookie sheets, if necessary. Bake 10 minutes or until golden. Transfer to wire rack to cool.

In small bowl combine cherry pie filling and amaretto or kirsch; mix well. On each of 6 dessert plates layer filling between 2 cookies and top with whipped topping.

CUTTING AND CHOPPING

Knowing the difference between mincing and dicing can help ensure successful results when following recipes.

- Chopped: *uneven pieces larger than ½ inch.*
- Cubed: *Square-sided pieces at least ½ inch in size.*
- Diced: *Square-sided pieces smaller than ½ inch in size.*
- Minced: *Chopped pieces that are very small and uneven.*

Beef Tournedos, page 62

Beef Tournedos

A CLASSIC COMPANY DINNER

From the tournedos and tiny carrots to the creamy mocha dessert, this is a menu to serve proudly to guests and family alike. These juicy flank steak pinwheels, fragrant with rosemary, go together quickly and cook in less than ten minutes.

══ Menu for 4 ══

- **Beef Tournedos**
  Buttered
  Noodles
- **Minted Baby**
  Carrots
  Green Salad
- **Mocha Whip**

SHOPPING LIST

- ☐ 1   pound flank steak
- ☐ 24-30   baby carrots
- ☐   Salad greens
- ☐ 1   bunch fresh mint or dried mint
- ☐ 1   12-ounce package mini chocolate chips
- ☐ 1   jar instant espresso coffee
- ☐ 1   package ladyfingers
- ☐ 1   15-ounce container ricotta cheese
- ☐ ½   pint heavy or whipping cream

Have on Hand

- ☐   Sugar
- ☐   Cocoa
- ☐   Egg noodles
- ☐   Salt

- ☐   Instant minced onion
- ☐   Rosemary
- ☐   Onion salt
- ☐   Unseasoned meat tenderizer
- ☐   Vanilla extract
- ☐   Bottled salad dressing
- ☐   Butter or margarine
- ☐   Bacon

SCHEDULE

1. Place flank steak in freezer.
2. Prepare Mocha Whip; refrigerate.
3. Cook Minted Baby Carrots.
4. Cook noodles.
5. Prepare salad.
6. Prepare Beef Tournedos.

Beef Tournedos

1 **pound flank steak**
1 **tablespoon instant minced onion**
1 **tablespoon water**
   Unseasoned meat tenderizer
½ **teaspoon crumbled rosemary**
¼ **teaspoon onion salt**
4 **strips bacon**

Place steak on cookie sheet in the freezer for 10 minutes.

Preheat broiler. Combine minced onion with water. With a sharp knife cut steak horizontally almost in half but without cutting all the way through. Open it up and press the fold flat. Sprinkle with meat tenderizer, rosemary and onion salt. Slicing across the grain, cut into 4 strips. Roll each strip jelly-roll style, wrapping each in a strip of bacon; secure with toothpick. Broil 5 to 8 minutes on each side about 4 inches from heat.

Minted Baby Carrots

24-30 **baby carrots, trimmed**
1 **teaspoon salt**
2 **tablespoons butter or margarine**
2 **teaspoons sugar**
1½ **tablespoons fresh chopped or 2 teaspoons dried mint**

In large saucepan combine carrots and salt with water to cover. Bring to a boil over high heat. Cook 20 minutes or until fork tender; drain. Return carrots to pan; add butter or margarine and sugar. Shake pan over low heat to melt butter and glaze carrots. Sprinkle with mint.

Mocha Whip

8 **ladyfingers, split lengthwise**
1 **cup heavy or whipping cream**
1 **teaspoon instant espresso coffee**
½ **teaspoon vanilla extract**
¾ **cup part-skim ricotta cheese**
3 **tablespoons sugar**
2 **tablespoons cocoa**
2 **tablespoons mini chocolate chips**
   Additional whipped cream (optional)

Line 4 dessert dishes with ladyfingers. In blender combine cream, instant coffee, vanilla, ricotta cheese, sugar and cocoa; blend until smooth. Stir in chocolate chips and spoon into serving dishes. Refrigerate until serving time; garnish with additional whipped cream if desired.

WHIPPED CREAM TIPS

• *For the fastest and frothiest results, keep the cream in the refrigerator until you're ready to whip it.*
• *Chill the beaters and a small bowl in the freezer.*

Bonus Bagels

For instant brunches, slice bagels in half, toast them and top them with:
- *Scrambled Eggs, Cheddar cheese and chopped green chilies.*
- *Heated rounds of corned beef hash topped with poached eggs.*

For lunch, slice them, toast them and top with:
- *Slices of onion, tomato and cheese, strips of cooked bacon. Broil until cheese is bubbly.*
- *Ham, pineapple ring, Muenster cheese and a spoonful of chutney.*
- *A split broiled frank, a heap of baked beans, a sprinkling of shredded Cheddar cheese, and a dollop of prepared mustard.*
- *Pizza sauce and shredded mozzarella cheese. Broil until cheese is melted.*
- *Slice of tomato, scoop of low-fat cottage cheese, strips of green pepper. Season with chives.*

Start with Instant Mashed Potatoes

A satisfying side dish, the easy spuds can also be used:
- *As an extender. Excellent to work into ground meat (2 tablespoons to 1 pound) for burgers, meat loaves, stuffed peppers. Toss some into a batch of omelets (1 tablespoon to 4 eggs) or to round out a spicy chili.*
- *As a topping. Combine ½ to 1 cup with 1 to 2 tablespoons melted butter or margarine and cover casseroles before baking.*

Quick Goodies from Refrigerated Biscuits

Pop open a package of this ready-made dough and whip up:
- Breakfast Danish—*Dip biscuits in melted butter or margarine. Make a thumbprint in each and fill the indentation with your favorite jam or jelly. Bake.*
- Sandwich Turnovers—*Press 2 biscuits together and roll out to a 6-inch circle. Fill center with tuna, ham salad, etc.; fold over, press edges and bake.*

Mushroom Magic

Start with a 10¾-oz. can of cream of mushroom soup for an easy trip from the mundane to the marvelous.

- *Vegetable Velvet: For a fast vegetable sauce blend a can of mushroom soup with ¼ cup milk and a 3-oz. square of cream cheese. Heat, stir, and pour over cooked vegetables before serving.*
- *Walnut Delight: Warm up a can of cream of mushroom soup with ¼ cup milk and chopped walnuts. Serve over roast chicken from the deli or leftover chicken.*
- *Dreamy Creamy Fettucini: Heat a can of cream of mushroom soup with ¾ cup milk and ½ cup grated Parmesan cheese; stir. Fold in steaming cooked fettucini and a generous dollop of butter. Serve immediately.*

Quick Dash with Nutmeg

In addition to the traditional seasonal sprinkle on eggnog, try using nutmeg these new ways:

- *Blend into butter or margarine for a savory complement to spinach.*
- *Grate fresh nutmeg into cider or beer—traditional in southern Germany.*
- *Perk up fish cakes, chowders or seafood casseroles with a hefty shake.*
- *Give a nutty taste to steaming hot cabbage wedges or broccoli spears.*
- *Add a dash to liven up the taste of plain spaghetti with butter.*

Quick Mexi-Cheese Bake

Preheat oven to 350° F. Prepare a 7¾ oz. package of macaroni and cheese dinner according to package directions; pour into baking dish. Stir in a can (6¾ oz.) of chunked ham and 2 tablespoons canned chopped green chilies. Top with 1 cup crushed tortilla chips; dot with butter. Bake until bubbly, about 15 minutes. Serves 4.

Spaghetti with Clam Sauce

HEARTY PASTA DINNER IN MINUTES

Homemade pasta sauce couldn't be easier to prepare and couldn't taste better no matter how much time you spent. A green salad and a creamy orange dessert round out this easy and delicious meal.

Menu for 4

- **Spaghetti with Clam Sauce Italian Bread**

Tossed Salad with
- **Creamy Garlic Dressing**
- **Orange Whip**

SHOPPING LIST

- ☐ 1 pound thin spaghetti
- ☐ 1 bunch fresh parsley
- ☐ Salad greens
- ☐ 3 6½-ounce cans minced clams
- ☐ 1 6-ounce can orange juice concentrate
- ☐ 1 11-ounce can mandarin oranges
- ☐ 1 loaf Italian bread
- ☐ 1 8-ounce container frozen whipped topping made with real cream
- ☐ 1 8-ounce container sour cream
- ☐ 1 8-ounce container vanilla yogurt

Have on Hand
- ☐ All-purpose flour
- ☐ Salt
- ☐ Pepper
- ☐ Garlic
- ☐ Crushed red pepper
- ☐ Olive oil
- ☐ Mayonnaise
- ☐ Milk
- ☐ Dry white wine

SCHEDULE

1. Prepare Orange Whip; place in freezer.
2. Heat water for spaghetti.
3. Prepare salad and Creamy Garlic Dressing.
4. Prepare Spaghetti with Clam Sauce.

Spaghetti with Clam Sauce

1   pound thin spaghetti
1/4 cup olive oil
2   garlic cloves, minced
1   tablespoon all-purpose
      flour
3   cans (6½-oz. each) minced
      clams, drained, juice
      reserved
1/3 cup dry white wine
1/4 teaspoon crushed red
      pepper
1/4 teaspoon salt
3   tablespoons chopped
      parsley

Cook spaghetti according to package directions. In medium saucepan heat oil. Add garlic and saute 2 minutes. Stir in flour. Add reserved clam juice, wine, red pepper flakes and salt. Bring to a boil and simmer 10 minutes. Add minced clams and parsley. Return to a boil and remove from heat. Serve sauce over hot drained spaghetti.

Creamy Garlic Dressing

2/3 cup sour cream
1/3 cup mayonnaise
1   tablespoon milk
      Dash pepper
1   garlic clove, crushed

In small bowl combine all ingredients; stir until smooth; refrigerate.

Orange Whip

1   cup vanilla yogurt
2   tablespoons orange juice
      concentrate, thawed
1   pint frozen whipped
      topping with real
      cream, thawed
1   can (11 oz.) mandarin
      oranges, drained

Blend yogurt and orange juice concentrate into whipped topping. Fold mandarin oranges into topping mixture. Spoon into individual serving bowls and place in freezer until serving time.

OTHER SOUR CREAM SALAD DRESSINGS

Vary the basic recipe given above by adding:
* *1 tablespoon mustard, 1/4 teaspoon dillweed and 1/8 teaspoon salt*
* *1/2 cup crumbled blue cheese, 1 teaspoon vinegar and dash salt*
* *3 tablespoons chili sauce, 2 tablespoons minced onion, 1 teaspoon Worcestershire sauce and 1/8 teaspoon salt*

Baked Eggs in Hash Cups

CORNED BEEF HASH 'N' EGGS

This hash-and-eggs entree makes a satisfying dinner or a hearty breakfast for a winter morning. You can make a similar dish with bulk sausage instead of hash, if you prefer. Either way, you can bake the muffins and the hash at the same time. For some easy variations on our basic recipe for Old-Fashioned Muffins, note the directions in the Tips section.

Menu for 4

- **Baked Eggs in Corned Beef Hash Cups**
- **Old-Fashioned Muffins Fruit Compote**

SHOPPING LIST

- ☐ 1 15- or 16-ounce can corned beef hash
- ☐ 1 medium onion
- ☐ 1 green pepper
- ☐ Fresh fruit or 1 20-ounce package frozen fruit
- ☐ 1 dozen eggs

- ☐ Salt
- ☐ Pepper
- ☐ Vanilla extract
- ☐ Ketchup
- ☐ Worcestershire sauce
- ☐ Butter or margarine
- ☐ Milk

Have on Hand

- ☐ All-purpose flour
- ☐ Sugar
- ☐ Baking powder
- ☐ Shortening
- ☐ Paprika

SCHEDULE

1. Prepare Old-Fashioned Muffins.
2. Prepare or thaw fruit for compote.
3. Prepare Baked Eggs in Corned Beef Hash Cups.

Baked Eggs in Corned Beef Hash Cups

3   tablespoons ketchup
1   tablespoon plus 1 teaspoon
      Worcestershire sauce
¼   teaspoon salt
⅛   teaspoon pepper
5   eggs
1   can (15 or 16 oz.) corned
      beef hash
⅔   cup chopped onion
½   cup chopped green pepper
      Paprika

Preheat oven to 400° F. In mixing bowl combine ketchup, Worcestershire sauce, salt, pepper and 1 egg, beaten. Add corned beef hash, onion and green pepper. Mix well. Put ⅓ cup corned beef hash mixture in each of four 10-ounce baking dishes. Make depressions in the hash for eggs. Bake 8 minutes. Break 1 egg into each hash cup; bake 5 minutes or until eggs are set. Sprinkle with paprika.

Old-Fashioned Muffins

2   cups all-purpose flour
½   cup sugar
2   teaspoons baking powder
1   teaspoon salt
¼   cup butter or margarine,
      softened
¼   cup shortening

½   cup milk
½   teaspoon vanilla extract
2   eggs, beaten

Preheat oven to 400° F. Grease twelve 2 ½-inch muffin-pan cups; set aside.

In medium bowl combine dry ingredients and mix well. Cut in butter and shortening until mixture resembles fine crumbs. Combine milk, vanilla and eggs. Add to dry ingredients all at once, stirring just until moistened. Spoon batter into prepared pan, filling each cup ¾ full. Bake 20 to 25 minutes, or until golden brown. Immediately remove from pan to wire rack.

VARIATIONS ON THE OLD-FASHIONED MUFFIN

To one basic Old-Fashioned Muffins recipe (above), along with the milk and eggs, add:

- *¾ cup chopped cranberries*
- *1 cup each finely chopped unpeeled apple and shredded Cheddar cheese*
- *1 ½ cups fresh or frozen blueberries (bake 30 to 35 minutes and cool 5 minutes in pan)*
- *1½ teaspoons grated lemon peel and ½ teaspoon ground cardamom*
- *½ cup flaked coconut and 2 teaspoons grated orange peel*

Rigatoni Italiano

ITALIAN DINNER WITH ONION BREAD

Any pasta would taste good here, but we've used broad rigatoni, an easy-to-handle alternative to spaghetti. Green pepper and onions add crunch and flavor to the sauce.

═══ Menu for 4 ═══

- **Rigatoni Italiano**
- **Fried Zucchini Strips**
- **Tossed Salad with Oil and Vinegar**
- **Green Onion Bread**
- **Angel Food Cake with Mixed Fruit**

SHOPPING LIST

- ☐ 1 pound beef cube steaks
- ☐ 1 16-ounce package rigatoni
- ☐ 1 onion
- ☐ 1 green pepper
- ☐ 4 small zucchini
- ☐ 1 bunch green onions
- ☐ Salad greens
- ☐ 1 15½-ounce jar spaghetti sauce
- ☐ 1 loaf Italian bread
- ☐ 1 angel food cake
- ☐ 1 20-ounce package frozen mixed fruit

Have on Hand

- ☐ All-purpose flour
- ☐ Salt
- ☐ Pepper
- ☐ Oregano
- ☐ Salad oil
- ☐ Vinegar
- ☐ Butter or margarine
- ☐ Parmesan Cheese

SCHEDULE

1. Thaw fruit.
2. Prepare Rigatoni Italiano.
3. Prepare salad.
4. Prepare Green Onion Bread.
5. Prepare Fried Zucchini Strips.

Rigatoni Italiano

1 pound rigatoni
2 tablespoons salad oil
1 pound beef cube steaks, cut into strips
1 onion, chopped
1 green pepper, cut into strips
1 jar (15½ oz.) spaghetti sauce
½ teaspoon salt
⅛ teaspoon pepper
Grated Parmesan cheese

Cook rigatoni according to package directions. Meanwhile, in large skillet heat salad oil. Add cube steak, onion and green pepper; saute. Stir in spaghetti sauce and salt and pepper. Cover and simmer 10 minutes. Serve over hot rigatoni with grated Parmesan.

Fried Zucchini Strips

2 tablespoons all-purpose flour
½ teaspoon salt
⅛ teaspoon pepper
¼ teaspoon oregano
4 small zucchini, halved lengthwise and cut into 2-inch strips
3 tablespoons salad oil

Place flour, salt, pepper and oregano in plastic bag; add zucchini strips, a few at a time, and shake well. In large skillet heat oil over medium heat. Add zucchini strips and cook 5 to 8 minutes, turning once, until golden brown.

Green Onion Bread

½ cup butter or margarine, softened
2 tablespoons chopped green onions
⅛ teaspoon pepper
1 loaf Italian bread

Preheat oven to 350° F. In small bowl combine butter or margarine, chopped green onions and pepper. Cut bread into 1-inch slices without cutting through bottom crust. Spread slices with green onion butter. Wrap loaf in foil and warm in oven 15 minutes or until heated through.

HOT BREAD TIPS

Try chopped chives instead of green onions for a variation on our Green Onion Bread. For other hot breads, to ½ cup butter add:
- *1 clove garlic, finely chopped*
- *1 tablespoon grated Romano or Parmesan cheese*
- *2 tablespoons finely chopped onion and a dash of Worcestershire sauce*

Sausage, Pepper and Potato Skillet

FAST AND TASTY DINNER IN A SKILLET

Meat, potatoes and vegetable cook together in this top-of-the-stove casserole, a recipe you'll want to keep in mind for cold weather brunches as well as for dinner. The unusual fruit dessert comes from Brazil, where sauteed bananas have long been a favorite.

Menu for 4

- **Sausage, Pepper and Potato Skillet Tossed Salad**
- **Garlic-Oregano Breadsticks**
- **Cartola**

SHOPPING LIST

- ☐ 1 pound Italian-style sausages
- ☐ Salad greens
- ☐ 1 bunch fresh or dried parsley
- ☐ 1 medium onion
- ☐ 1 green pepper
- ☐ 1 red pepper
- ☐ 4 medium potatoes
- ☐ 4 bananas
- ☐ 1 loaf unsliced white bread
- ☐ 4 ounces Muenster cheese
- ☐ Fresh or frozen strawberries (optional)

Have on Hand
- ☐ Salt
- ☐ Pepper

- ☐ Garlic
- ☐ Oregano
- ☐ Cinnamon sugar
- ☐ Bottled salad dressing
- ☐ Butter or margarine

SCHEDULE

1. Prepare Sausage, Pepper and Potato Skillet.
2. Prepare Garlic-Oregano Breadsticks.
3. Prepare salad.
4. Prepare Cartola.

Sausage, Pepper and Potato Skillet

1   pound Italian-style sausage
1   medium onion
1   green pepper
1   red pepper
4   medium potatoes
³⁄₄ cup water
1   teaspoon salt
¹⁄₈ teaspoon pepper

Cut sausage into 1-inch chunks. In large skillet brown on all sides. Meanwhile, cut onion, peppers and potatoes into 1-inch chunks. Drain excess drippings from browned sausage; add remaining ingredients. Cover and cook over low heat 15 to 20 minutes, until potatoes are fork tender.

Garlic-Oregano Breadsticks

¹⁄₄ cup butter or margarine
¹⁄₂ loaf unsliced white bread,
      crust removed
2   tablespoons chopped parsley
2   teaspoons crumbled oregano
1   garlic clove, minced

Preheat oven to 350° F. Place butter or margarine in 9-inch square baking pan and set in oven to melt. Cut bread crosswise into thirds; halve each piece from top to bottom and then cut each chunk into 3 equal-size sticks. Stir parsley, oregano and garlic into melted butter in baking pan. Place breadsticks in pan;

turn to coat with butter mixture. Bake 15 minutes until crisp and browned.

Cartola

2   tablespoons butter
4   bananas
4   slices Muenster cheese
    Cinnamon sugar
    Strawberries (optional)

Preheat oven to 350° F. In medium skillet melt butter. Add bananas and saute until tender. Wrap each in a slice of Muenster cheese and place on ungreased cookie sheet. Sprinkle with cinnamon sugar and bake in oven until cheese is slightly melted, about 6 minutes. Garnish with strawberries and serve immediately.

ITALIAN SAUSAGE TIPS

- *For a quick and hearty feast, serve mild or hot Italian sausages, sliced and browned, with rigatoni or ziti and bottled marinara sauce.*
- *Remove 1 pound Italian sausage meat from casing and cook thoroughly; stir in ³⁄₄ cup bread crumbs, ¹⁄₄ cup milk and 1 lightly beaten egg. Spoon sausage mixture into cooked and drained large pasta such as manicotti. Place stuffed pasta in baking dish; pour on 4 cups prepared spaghetti sauce, sprinkle with grated Parmesan cheese and bake at 400° F. for 25 to 30 minutes until heated through.*

Quick Veal Parmigiana

VEAL PARMIGIANA WITH A SURPRISE SOUP

Frozen veal patties and prepared marinara sauce make this Italian dish as fast as it is delicious. For a flavor surprise, make the smooth soup with cucumbers instead of zucchini. We think you'll find our Orange Cream a tasty complement to almost any fresh fruit.

Menu for 4

- **Zucchini Soup**
- **Quick Veal Parmigiana Lettuce and Red Onion Salad**

  Hard Rolls
- **Seedless Grapes and Bananas with Orange Cream**

SHOPPING LIST

- ☐ 1 red onion
- ☐ 1 yellow or white onion
- ☐ 1 head romaine lettuce
- ☐ 2 large or 4 small zucchini
- ☐ 1 bunch fresh dill or dillweed
- ☐ 1 orange
- ☐ 1 large bunch seedless grapes
- ☐ 4 bananas
- ☐ 1 15½-ounce jar marinara sauce
- ☐ 1 13¾- or 14½-ounce can chicken broth
- ☐ ½ pound mozzarella cheese
- ☐ 1 8-ounce container frozen whipped topping with real cream
- ☐ 4 frozen breaded veal patties

Have on Hand

- ☐ Salt
- ☐ Pepper
- ☐ Wine vinegar
- ☐ Butter or margarine
- ☐ Grated Parmesan cheese
- ☐ Orange liqueur

SCHEDULE

1. Prepare Zucchini Soup.
2. Prepare Quick Veal Parmigiana.
3. Assemble salad.
4. Prepare Seedless Grapes and Bananas with Orange Cream.

Zucchini Soup

¼ cup butter or margarine
1 onion, chopped
2 cups sliced zucchini
1¾ cups chicken broth
2 tablespoons wine vinegar
1 tablespoon fresh dill or 1
    teaspoon dillweed
½ teaspoon salt
    Dash pepper

In large saucepot melt butter or margarine; add onion and saute until translucent. Add zucchini, broth, vinegar, dill and salt and pepper. Bring to a boil; lower heat and simmer 20 minutes. Puree in blender until smooth.

Quick Veal Parmigiana

4 frozen breaded veal patties
1 jar (15½ oz.) marinara
    sauce
½ pound mozzarella cheese,
    sliced or shredded
½ cup grated Parmesan
    cheese

Preheat oven to 350° F. Prepare veal patties according to package directions for pan-frying. In lightly greased baking dish, layer veal, marinara sauce, mozzarella and Parmesan. Cover loosely with foil; bake 15 minutes. Uncover, bake 5 minutes longer.

Seedless Grapes and Bananas with Orange Cream

1 large bunch seedless grapes
4 bananas, sliced
¾ cup frozen whipped top-
    ping with real cream
3 tablespoons orange liqueur
1 teaspoon grated orange
    peel

Divide grapes and sliced bananas among 4 dessert bowls. In small bowl combine whipped topping, liqueur and orange peel. Spoon Orange Cream over fruit.

ZUCCHINI QUICKIES

Its subtle taste and ease of preparation make the zucchini one of our most versatile vegetables:
- *Slice a raw zucchini and toss into green salad.*
- *Coarsely grate zucchini and carrots or yellow squash, cook in butter or margarine 3 to 4 minutes. Season with salt and pepper.*
- *Halve zucchini lengthwise, scoop out seeds and blanch 5 minutes. Fill with chopped tomato and diced cheese. Top with partially cooked bacon or seasoned bread crumbs. Broil until cheese is melted.*

Chili Omelet

WINTER OMELET WITH VARIATIONS

Make this Mexican-accented omelet with leftover or canned chili, or try the frozen kind that comes in a tube. Our Tips section provides you with ideas for your next omelet meal.

=== **Menu for 4** ===

- **Chili Omelet**
- **Mushroom and Bibb Lettuce Salad**
- **Toasted Pita Breads**
- **Fruit Rainbow**

SHOPPING LIST

☐	1	15-ounce can chili
☐	1	small onion
☐	3	heads Bibb or Boston lettuce
☐		Pita breads
☐	¼	pound mushrooms
☐	1	16- or 17-ounce can apricot halves
☐	1	11-ounce can mandarin oranges
☐	1	8-ounce can pineapple chunks
☐	1	small can or package shredded coconut
☐	1	package miniature marshmallows
☐	1	4-ounce package shredded Cheddar cheese
☐	1	16-ounce container sour cream
☐	1	dozen eggs

Have on Hand

☐	Salt
☐	Pepper
☐	Garlic
☐	Thyme
☐	Bay leaves
☐	Capers
☐	Salad oil
☐	White vinegar
☐	Butter or margarine

SCHEDULE

1. Prepare salad and dressing; refrigerate.
2. Prepare Fruit Rainbow.
3. Toast pita breads.
4. Prepare Chili Omelets.

Chili Omelet

8	eggs
1/2	cup water, divided
1/2	teaspoon salt, divided
1/8	teaspoon pepper, divided
4	tablespoons butter or margarine, divided
1	cup shredded Cheddar cheese, divided
1 1/2	cups prepared chili, heated and divided
1/2	cup sour cream (optional)
1/2	cup chopped onion (optional)

Prepare two 4-egg omelets: For each omelet, in small bowl combine 4 eggs, 1/4 cup water and salt and pepper. In omelet pan or skillet melt 2 tablespoons butter or margarine. As soon as it begins to sizzle, pour in eggs. Push cooked eggs from edges to center of pan with pancake turner. Tilt pan to let uncooked egg flow underneath. While omelet is still creamy and moist on top, fill one side with half the cheese; spoon on half of the chili. With pancake turner, flip unfilled side over one third of the omelet. Loosen omelet and ease onto warmed plate; cut in half. Top with sour cream and chopped onion, if desired.

Mushroom and Bibb Lettuce Salad

1/2	cup salad oil
5	tablespoons white vinegar
1	large clove garlic, finely minced
1/2	teaspoon thyme
1	bay leaf
3	heads Bibb or Boston lettuce
1/2	cup sliced fresh mushrooms
2	tablespoons capers, drained

In small jar with tight-fitting lid combine oil, vinegar, garlic, thyme and bay leaf. Cover and shake well; set aside. Remove bay leaf before serving.

Wash, drain and tear lettuce. Toss with mushrooms and capers. Add dressing and toss again.

Fruit Rainbow

1	can (16 or 17 oz.) apricot halves, drained and cut into chunks
1	can (11 oz.) mandarin oranges, drained
1	can (8 oz.) pineapple chunks, drained
1	cup shredded coconut
1	cup sour cream
1	cup miniature marshmallows

In large bowl combine all ingredients. Stir gently until well blended. Cover and chill until serving time.

OMELETS: FILL 'EM WITH . . .

- *Prepared avocado dip and bacon bits*
- *Zucchini in tomato sauce, grated Parmesan cheese*
- *Canned deviled ham, mushrooms*
- *Frozen creamed chicken, curry powder, chutney*

Land's End Chowder

WARMING AND WONDERFUL SEAFOOD MEAL

This tasty and nutritious chowder cooks in minutes, yet is delicious enough for special occasions. Oyster crackers are the traditional accompaniment, and always, a cool green salad or cole slaw. A warm and hearty meal in fall or winter, this chowder is also popular in the summer because it requires little time at the stove.

Menu for 4

- **Land's End Chowder Oyster Crackers**

- **Spinach Salad Cherry Pie**

SHOPPING LIST

- ☐ 1 pound bacon
- ☐ 1 medium onion
- ☐ 2 medium potatoes
- ☐ 1 pound fresh spinach
- ☐ ¼ pound fresh mushrooms
- ☐ 1 16-ounce can whole kernel corn
- ☐ 1 5⅓-ounce can evaporated milk
- ☐ 1 box oyster crackers
- ☐ Cherry pie
- ☐ 2 ounces blue cheese
- ☐ 1 16-ounce package frozen cod fillets

Have on Hand

- ☐ Salt
- ☐ Pepper
- ☐ 1 lemon or lemon juice
- ☐ Olive oil
- ☐ Salad oil
- ☐ Butter or margarine

SCHEDULE

1. Prepare Spinach Salad and dressing; refrigerate.
2. Prepare Land's End Chowder.

Land's End Chowder

3   *slices bacon, cut into*
      ½-inch pieces
1   *medium onion, sliced*
2   *medium potatoes, peeled*
      and cubed
2½ *cups hot water*
1½ *teaspoons salt*
¼   *teaspoon pepper*
1   *package (16 oz.) frozen*
      cod fillets
1   *can (16 oz.) whole kernel*
      corn
1   *can (5⅓ oz.) evaporated*
      milk
2   *tablespoons butter or*
      margarine

In large saucepan cook bacon until crisp; remove and drain. Add onion to bacon drippings and saute until tender. Add potatoes, water, salt and pepper. Bring to boil over medium heat. Cover; reduce heat and simmer until potatoes are tender but still firm. Add frozen fish; cover and cook 8 to 10 minutes, stirring until fish breaks up easily. Stir in corn and milk. Cover and cook until heated through. Ladle into individual bowls. Top each serving with a pat of butter and a sprinkling of bacon.

Spinach Salad

1   *pound spinach, washed,*
      trimmed and coarsely
      torn
¼   *pound fresh mushrooms,*
      sliced
½   *cup crumbled cooked*
      bacon (about 10 slices)
2   *ounces crumbled blue*
      cheese
¼   *cup olive oil*
¼   *cup salad oil*
¼   *cup water*
3   *tablespoons lemon juice*
¾   *teaspoon salt*
⅛   *teaspoon pepper*

In large bowl combine spinach, mushrooms, half the bacon and half the cheese. In small jar with tight-fitting lid combine oils, water, lemon juice, salt and pepper. Cover and shake well. Pour over salad and toss. Sprinkle with remaining bacon and cheese.

CRUMBLED BACON TIPS

Cook 3 or 4 slices of bacon until crisp. Drain well and crumble. Scatter over:
- *Cooked green beans, Brussels sprouts or cauliflower*
- *Baked potatoes with sour cream*
- *Any fresh green salad*
- *Welsh rarebit on toast*
- *Macaroni and cheese*
- *Roast beef slices for sandwiches*

Country Sausage with Winter Fruit

A HEARTY AND COLORFUL ENTREE

This appealing and delicious entree will be ready in minutes. If you're entertaining, you can cook the sausage ahead and keep it warm. We used slivered almonds in our green bean recipe, but pine nuts are good, too, so use them if you have some on hand.

Menu for 4

- **Country Sausage with Winter Fruit Whole Wheat Rolls**

- **Green Beans with Slivered Almonds Spice Cake**

SHOPPING LIST

- ☐ 1   16-ounce package bulk sausage
- ☐ 1½ pounds fresh green beans
- ☐ 1   large red apple
- ☐ 1   large pear
- ☐ 1   small papaya
- ☐ 1   small can or package slivered almonds
- ☐   Whole wheat rolls
- ☐ 1   spice cake

Have on Hand
- ☐   Sugar
- ☐   Salt

- ☐   Cinnamon
- ☐ 1   lemon or lemon juice
- ☐   Butter or margarine
- ☐   Calvados, apple jack or brandy

SCHEDULE

1. Prepare Green Beans with Slivered Almonds.
2. Prepare Country Sausage and Winter Fruit.

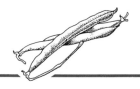

Country Sausage with Winter Fruit

1   large red apple, cored and sliced
1   large pear, cored and sliced
1   teaspoon lemon juice
2   teaspoons sugar
¼   teaspoon cinnamon
¼   cup calvados, apple jack or brandy
1   package (16 oz.) bulk sausage
2   tablespoons butter or margarine
    Dash salt
1   small papaya, sliced

In large bowl toss apple and pear slices with lemon juice, sugar, cinnamon and calvados. Cut sausage into ½-inch slices. In saucepot saute sausage until browned and cooked through; drain off fat. Remove sausage; keep warm. In same pot melt butter or margarine; stir in fruit mixture and salt. Toss gently; cook over high heat about 2 minutes. Reduce heat; add papaya and cook about 2 minutes more, stirring gently. Add sausage and heat through.

Green Beans with Slivered Almonds

1½   pounds fresh green beans
½   teaspoon salt
3   tablespoons butter
¼   cup slivered almonds, toasted

Trim beans and snap in half. In saucepot heat to boiling enough water to cover beans. Add salt and beans; return to boil and cook uncovered 12 to 15 minutes or just until tender-crisp. Drain. Add butter and toss beans until butter melts. Sprinkle with toasted almonds.

PINE NUTS OR SLIVERED ALMONDS FOR QUICK CRUNCH

- *Spread pine nuts or slivered almonds in a flat baking dish lined with foil. Toast in a 350° F. oven for 5 to 7 minutes, shaking pan once or twice, until lightly toasted.*
- *Scatter on cooked green vegetables or broiled or baked white-fleshed fish.*
- *Add to fresh green salad or sprinkle on ice cream or puddings.*

Chopped Beef Rolls

A NEW TREATMENT FOR AN OLD FAVORITE

Let's face it, Americans love hamburgers. This variation, cooked in the broiler and flavored with chili sauce, is sure to become a family standard. In addition to our recipe for peachy baked beans, here are some tasty tips on using canned peaches.

Menu for 4

- **Chopped Beef Rolls**
- **Baked Beans with Peaches**
- **Lettuce Wedges with Thousand Island Dressing**
- **Pound Cake with Strawberries**

SHOPPING LIST

- ☐ 1 head iceberg lettuce
- ☐ 1 16-ounce can peach slices in heavy syrup
- ☐ 1 16-ounce can pork and beans in tomato sauce
- ☐ 1 bottle Thousand Island dressing
- ☐ Pound cake
- ☐ 1 8-ounce container sour cream
- ☐ 1 package frozen strawberries
- ☐ 1 pound lean ground beef

Have on Hand
- ☐ Sugar
- ☐ Salt
- ☐ Cinnamon
- ☐ Dry mustard

- ☐ Chili sauce
- ☐ Bread crumbs
- ☐ Horseradish
- ☐ Maple syrup
- ☐ Eggs

SCHEDULE

1. Place frozen strawberries at room temperature to thaw.
2. Prepare Baked Beans with Peaches.
3. Cook Chopped Beef Rolls.
4. Prepare salad.
5. Prepare dessert.

Chopped Beef Rolls

1   pound lean ground beef
¾   cup chili sauce, divided
¼   cup dry bread crumbs
1   egg, beaten
1   teaspoon salt
1   teaspoon horseradish,
         drained
¼   teaspoon dry mustard

In medium bowl combine ground beef, ½ cup chili sauce, bread crumbs, egg, salt, horseradish and mustard until well mixed. Preheat broiler. Divide meat mixture into 8 equal parts. Shape each part into a 4-x-1 ½-inch cylinder. Place meat rolls on broiler pan so that they don't touch each other. Brush with some of the remaining chili sauce. Broil 4 inches from heat for 4 minutes. Turn, brush with remaining chili sauce. Broil 4 more minutes or until done to taste.

Baked Beans with Peaches

1   can (16 oz.) peach slices,
         drained
1   can (16 oz.) pork and
         beans in tomato sauce
1   tablespoon maple syrup
½   teaspoon cinnamon
½   teaspoon dry mustard

Preheat oven to 350° F. Pour peaches into a 1-quart casserole. Add pork and beans, maple syrup, cinnamon and dry mustard.

Stir to combine thoroughly. Bake 20 minutes or until heated through.

Pound Cake with Strawberries

1   container (8 oz.) sour cream
1   teaspoon sugar
     Pound cake slices
1   cup frozen strawberries,
         thawed

In small bowl combine sour cream and sugar. Place 1 slice of pound cake in each dessert dish. Spoon strawberries on top. Add sweetened sour cream.

START WITH A CAN OF PEACHES . . .

Drain a 16-ounce can of peach halves and:

- *Top with butter and lemon juice; broil until lightly browned. Serve with ham steaks, broiled chicken or pork chops.*
- *Fill with chutney and chopped peanuts and serve with curry.*
- *Arrange in buttered baking dish. Top with sour cream and sprinkle with brown sugar. Bake at 350° F. for 10 minutes.*

Honey-Mustard Chicken

CHICKEN DINNER WITH HOMEMADE SOUP

Making your own soup is no longer a full day's work. Our cauliflower soup goes together in minutes. See the Tip that follows for another quick soup.

Menu for 4

- **Cream of Cauliflower Soup**
- **Honey-Mustard Chicken**
- **Carrot-Zucchini Julienne**
  Apple Turnovers

SHOPPING LIST

- ☐ 2 2½-pound broiler-fryer chickens, halved
- ☐ 1 bunch celery
- ☐ 1 pound carrots
- ☐ 2 medium zucchini
- ☐ 1 lime
- ☐ 1 13¾- or 14½-ounce can chicken broth
- ☐ 1 package apple turnovers
- ☐ 2 10-ounce packages frozen cauliflower

Have on Hand

- ☐ Salt
- ☐ Garlic salt
- ☐ Pepper
- ☐ Ginger

- ☐ Curry powder
- ☐ Chives
- ☐ All-purpose flour
- ☐ Dijon mustard
- ☐ Butter or margarine
- ☐ Milk
- ☐ Honey

SCHEDULE

1. Prepare Cream of Cauliflower Soup; keep warm.
2. Cook Honey-Mustard Chicken.
3. Prepare Carrot-Zucchini Julienne.

Cream of Cauliflower Soup

2   packages (10 oz. each)
     frozen cauliflower
1/3 cup chopped celery
1/2 teaspoon curry powder
1/2 teaspoon salt
1   can (13¾ or 14½ oz.)
     chicken broth
3   tablespoons butter or
     margarine
3   tablespoons flour
2½   cups milk
     Chopped chives

In large saucepan cook cauliflower with celery, curry powder, salt and chicken broth, according to package directions. Puree in blender or food processor. Strain, if desired, and set aside. Melt butter or margarine in the same saucepan. Stir in flour and cook, stirring constantly with wire whisk until smooth and bubbly, about 1 minute. Slowly blend in milk. Bring just to a boil, stirring frequently. Stir in pureed cauliflower mixture and heat through. Garnish with chives.

Honey-Mustard Chicken

2   teaspoons garlic salt
2   broiler-fryer chickens (about
     2½ pounds each), halved
4   tablespoons Dijon mustard
     Juice of 1 lime
1/3 cup honey

Preheat broiler. Sprinkle garlic salt evenly on chicken halves. Place chicken on broiling pan, skin side down. Spread each half with ½ tablespoon mustard. Stir lime juice into honey; set aside. Broil chicken 5 inches from heat in gas broiler, 6 to 7 inches from heat in electric broiler, 15 minutes. Brush lime-honey mixture on chicken and broil 5 more minutes. Turn; spread other side with remaining mustard, broil 5 minutes or until tender. Baste with lime-honey mixture.

Carrot-Zucchini Julienne

2   tablespoons butter or
     margarine
2   medium zucchini, julienned
4   carrots, julienned
1/2 teaspoon salt
1/8 teaspoon pepper
     Dash ground ginger

In medium skillet melt butter or margarine; saute vegetables until tender. Add salt, pepper and ginger; stir to combine..

QUICK SPINACH SOUP TIP

For speedy spinach soup, follow the procedure for Cream of Cauliflower Soup, using 2 packages frozen chopped spinach, 2 tablespoons chopped onion, ½ teaspoon salt, ¼ teaspoon nutmeg, 1 cup water, 3 tablespoons each butter and flour and 2½ cups milk. Garnish with grated lemon peel.

Chopped Steak Diane

HEARTY TOP-OF-THE-STOVE BEEF DINNER

Here is a quickie version of the classic Steak Diane, made with fast-cooking ground beef and a sauce of brandy and shallots. Serve it with golden-brown Sauteed Potatoes, green beans with mushrooms and crusty French bread. End the meal with a quick, delicious dessert flavored with Amaretto.

Menu for 4

- **Chopped Steak Diane**
- **Sauteed Potatoes**
- **French Bread**
- **Green Beans with Mushrooms**
- **Sliced Peaches with Amaretto**

SHOPPING LIST

- ☐ 3 medium potatoes
- ☐ 2 large shallots
- ☐ 1 bunch fresh parsley
- ☐ French bread
- ☐ 1 Fresh peaches or frozen sliced peaches
- ☐ 1 package frozen green beans with mushrooms
- ☐ 1 pound lean ground beef

Have on Hand
- ☐ Salt
- ☐ Pepper
- ☐ Worcestershire sauce
- ☐ Salad oil
- ☐ Butter or margarine
- ☐ Amaretto
- ☐ Brandy

SCHEDULE

1. Prepare Sauteed Potatoes.
2. Cook Steak Diane.
3. Prepare vegetable.
4. Prepare dessert.

Chopped Steak Diane

5 tablespoons butter or
    margarine, divided
1/3 cup finely chopped shallots
1 pound lean ground beef
3/4 teaspoon salt
1 teaspoon Worcestershire
    sauce
1/8 teaspoon pepper
1/3 cup brandy
1 tablespoon chopped parsley
1 tablespoon water

In large skillet melt 1 tablespoon butter or margarine; cook shallots until tender but not brown. Reserve 1 tablespoon shallots for sauce; set aside.

In medium bowl combine remaining shallots with beef, salt, Worcestershire sauce and pepper; mix well. Shape into 4 oval patties. Melt 2 tablespoons butter in skillet over medium-high heat. Add meat and brown 3 to 4 minutes on each side for rare, 4 to 5 minutes on each side for medium, turning once. Transfer meat to serving dish. Discard drippings in skillet, but leave brown bits. Add brandy, parsley, water and reserved shallots to skillet. Cook sauce, scraping up brown bits. Boil 1 minute, stirring. Add remaining 2 tablespoons butter and stir until melted. Pour sauce over patties.

Sauteed Potatoes

3 medium potatoes, cut into
    3/4-inch cubes
2 tablespoons salad oil
1 tablespoon butter or
    margarine
1/2 teaspoon salt
1/8 teaspoon pepper

Pat potatoes dry with paper towels. In heavy skillet heat oil and butter or margarine. Add potatoes, turning to coat. Saute over medium-high heat, tossing occasionally with spoon, about 10 minutes or until potatoes begin to brown. Sprinkle with salt and pepper. Reduce heat to medium. Toss again. Cover and cook about 15 more minutes, tossing occasionally, until potatoes are golden and cooked through.

HOW TO PERK UP SAUTEED POTATOES

- *For extra flavor, cook finely chopped onion in butter until translucent; add potatoes and proceed as usual.*
- *Crumble crisp bacon over potatoes before serving.*
- *For a hearty breakfast, add 4 eggs to skillet when potatoes are almost finished; stir constantly until eggs are cooked to your taste.*

Tuna Rockefeller

A NEW AND DIFFERENT TUNA CASSEROLE

The inspiration for this tasty variation on the tuna casserole came from the famous Oysters Rockefeller, which are served on a bed of spinach.

═══ Menu for 4 ═══

- **Baked Stuffed Mushrooms**
- **Tuna Rockefeller**

- **Golden Velvet Baby Carrots**
- **Parker House Rolls**

Lemon Sherbet with Blueberries

SHOPPING LIST

- ☐ 2   7-ounce cans tuna
- ☐ 1   16-ounce can baby carrots
- ☐ 16   large mushrooms
- ☐ 1   bunch fresh parsley or dried parsley
- ☐ 1   small onion
- ☐ 1   package oven-ready Parker House rolls
- ☐ 1   12-ounce package frozen blueberries
- ☐ 2   10-ounce packages frozen chopped spinach
- ☐ 2   7-ounce packages frozen small onions in cream sauce
- ☐ 1   pint lemon sherbet

Have on Hand
- ☐   Salt

- ☐   Pepper
- ☐   Dry bread crumbs
- ☐   Cinnamon
- ☐   Nutmeg
- ☐   Vanilla extract
- ☐   Butter or margarine
- ☐   Orange juice concentrate

SCHEDULE

1. Prepare Baked Stuffed Mushrooms.
2. Prepare Tuna Rockefeller.
3. Prepare Golden Velvet Baby Carrots.
4. Bake oven-ready Parker House rolls.

Baked Stuffed Mushrooms

16 *large mushrooms*
2 *tablespoons chopped parsley*
¼ *cup dry bread crumbs*
2 *tablespoons grated onion*
¼ *teaspoon salt*
⅛ *teaspoon pepper*
3 *tablespoons butter or margarine*

Preheat oven to 350° F. Remove stems from mushrooms and mince. In small bowl combine stems, parsley, bread crumbs, onion, salt and pepper. Fill each cap with about 1 tablespoon bread crumb mixture; arrange in greased baking pan and dot each cap with about ½ teaspoon butter or margarine.

Tuna Rockefeller

2 *packages (10 oz. each) frozen chopped spinach*
¼ *teaspoon salt*
¼ *teaspoon nutmeg*
2 *packages (7 oz. each) frozen small onions in cream sauce*
2 *cans (7 oz. each) tuna, drained*

Preheat oven to 350° F. In medium saucepan cook frozen spinach in about ½ cup water with salt to taste until it is almost thawed; drain thoroughly. Place in shallow baking dish and sprinkle with nutmeg. Cook frozen onions according to package directions; add tuna and heat through. Pour onion and tuna on top of spinach in casserole. Bake 15 to 20 minutes.

Golden Velvet Baby Carrots

1½ *tablespoons butter or margarine*
1 *can (16 oz.) whole baby carrots*
4 *tablespoons cup frozen orange juice concentrate, thawed*
¼ *cup water*
¼ *teaspoon vanilla extract*
¼ *teaspoon cinnamon*

Melt butter or margarine in top of double boiler over hot water. Pour into blender container. Add about 3 carrots, orange juice concentrate, water, vanilla and cinnamon. Puree until smooth. Pour into top of double boiler. Add remaining carrots and stir. Cover and cook until heated through.

QUICK DASH WITH NUTMEG

Nutmeg adds flavor to many dishes besides Tuna Rockefeller.

• *Add a dash to meatballs for a Swedish touch.*
• *Experiment with a pinch in beef stew to pick up the flavor.*
• *Mix a bit into pie dough for a seasoned shell.*
• *Stir ¼ teaspoon into creamed or whole-kernel corn.*

Reuben Casserole

HEARTY GERMAN-STYLE SUPPER IN 30 MINUTES

*Start this flavorful meal with a creamy carrot soup.
Then bring on the corned beef and sauerkraut casserole with a loaf of hearty beefsteak rye and a pitcher
of beer. Pickles complement this casserole; garlicky
half-sour dills taste great with corned beef.*

Menu for 4

- **Cream of Carrot Soup**
- **Reuben Casserole**

Rye Bread with Butter
Celery, Radishes and Pickles
Apple Strudel

SHOPPING LIST

- ☐ 1 12-ounce can corned beef or ¾ pound deli corned beef
- ☐ 2 pounds sauerkraut
- ☐ 1 onion
- ☐ 1 bunch celery
- ☐ 1 bunch radishes
- ☐ 1 bunch fresh parsley or dried parsley
- ☐ 1 bunch fresh dill or dillweed
- ☐ 1 13¾- or 14½-ounce can chicken broth
- ☐ 1 bottle Thousand Island dressing
- ☐ 1 loaf rye bread
- ☐   Apple strudel
- ☐ 1 package Swiss cheese slices
- ☐ 2 10-ounce packages frozen sliced carrots

Have on Hand

- ☐   All-purpose flour
- ☐   Salt
- ☐   Caraway seed
- ☐   Pickles
- ☐   Milk
- ☐   Butter or margarine

SCHEDULE

1. Prepare Reuben Casserole.
2. Cook Cream of Carrot Soup.
3. Prepare celery and radishes.

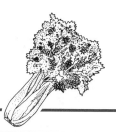

Cream of Carrot Soup

2 packages (10 oz. each)
    frozen sliced carrots
¼ cup chopped onion
2 tablespoons fresh dill or
    1½ teaspoons dillweed
¾ teaspoon salt
1 cup chicken broth
3 tablespoons butter or
    margarine
3 tablespoons flour
3½ cups milk
    Dill sprigs (optional)

In medium saucepan cook frozen carrots with onion, dill and salt. Puree with chicken broth in blender or food processor. Strain, if desired, and set aside.

In same saucepan melt butter or margarine. With wire whisk stir in flour and cook, stirring constantly, until smooth and bubbly, about 1 minute. Slowly blend in milk. Bring just to a boil, stirring frequently with whisk. Stir in pureed carrots and heat through. Garnish with dill sprigs, if desired.

Reuben Casserole

4 cups (2 lbs.) sauerkraut,
    rinsed and drained
1 teaspoon caraway seed
1 can (12 oz.) corned beef or
    ¾ pound deli corned
    beef, sliced
⅓ cup bottled Thousand
    Island dressing
1 package (4 oz.) sliced
    Swiss cheese
2 slices rye bread, toasted
    and cubed
2 tablespoons chopped
    parsley

Preheat oven to 350° F. Spread sauerkraut in shallow baking dish; sprinkle on caraway seed. Arrange corned beef on sauerkraut; spoon on dressing. Top with Swiss cheese. Sprinkle bread cubes over dish. Bake about 20 minutes, until hot. Garnish with parsley.

ANOTHER QUICK CREAMED SOUP

To make Cream of Artichoke Soup, just follow the procedure for Cream of Carrot Soup, using 2 packages frozen artichokes, 1 garlic clove, 2 teaspoons lemon juice, salt and pepper, 2 cups chicken broth, 3 tablespoons each butter and flour and 2 cups milk.

Linguine with Parsley-Tuna Sauce

ITALIAN PERFECTION WITH OVEN-PERFECT BREAD

Pasta is fast, easy and nourishing—perfect for family dinners or drop-in guests. Keep our Oregano Cheese Loaf in mind for a soup and salad dinner.

Menu for 4

- **Linguine with Parsley-Tuna Sauce**
- **Oregano Cheese Loaf**

Green Salad with Marinated Artichoke Hearts

Italian Pastries

SHOPPING LIST

- ☐ 1 16-ounce package linguine
- ☐ 1 large onion
- ☐ 1 bunch fresh parsley
- ☐ Salad greens
- ☐ 1 lemon or lemon juice
- ☐ 2 13-ounce cans evaporated milk
- ☐ 2 7-ounce cans tuna
- ☐ 1 jar marinated artichoke hearts
- ☐ 1 small jar pimientos
- ☐ 1 loaf French or Italian bread
- ☐ 1 8-ounce package Swiss cheese
- ☐ Italian pastries

- ☐ Oregano
- ☐ Garlic
- ☐ Worcestershire sauce
- ☐ Vinegar
- ☐ Butter or margarine
- ☐ Mayonnaise
- ☐ Sherry

Have on Hand

- ☐ All-purpose flour
- ☐ Salt

SCHEDULE

1. Prepare Oregano Cheese Loaf.
2. Cook linguine.
3. Prepare salad greens.
4. Prepare Linguine with Parsley-Tuna Sauce.

Linguine with Parsley-Tuna Sauce

1   package (16 oz.) linguine
2   tablespoons butter or margarine
½   cup chopped onion
2   garlic cloves, crushed
2   tablespoons flour
2   cans (13 oz.) each evaporated milk
¾   teaspoon salt
½   teaspoon Worcestershire sauce
2   cans tuna (6½ or 7 oz. each), drained
2   tablespoons lemon juice
3   tablespoons chopped parsley
2   tablespoons dry sherry (optional)
2   tablespoons diced pimiento

Cook linguine according to package directions.

Meanwhile, melt butter or margarine in a skillet and saute onion and garlic until translucent. Blend in flour and cook for 1 minute. Remove from heat and stir in evaporated milk, salt and Worcestershire sauce. Return to heat and cook, stirring constantly, until thickened. Mix in tuna and lemon juice. Simmer 3 to 5 minutes. Add parsley and sherry. Serve tuna sauce over linguine. Garnish with pimiento.

Oregano Cheese Loaf

2   cups (8 oz.) grated Swiss cheese
⅓   cup mayonnaise
1   tablespoon chopped fresh oregano or ½ teaspoon dried
1   tablespoon grated onion
1   tablespoon vinegar
1   loaf French or Italian bread

Preheat oven to 350° F. In medium bowl combine Swiss cheese, mayonnaise, oregano, onion and vinegar. Cut a lengthwise slice from top of bread and reserve. Pull soft crumbs out of bottom of loaf; fill loaf with cheese mixture and replace top.

Wrap filled loaf in foil. Bake 25 minutes. Cut into ¾-inch slices.

PRETTY IT UP WITH PIMIENTOS

Besides garnishing your linguine, you can use pimiento to:
- *Put a touch of color into scrambled eggs.*
- *Mince and stir into biscuit dough.*
- *Slash French bread and put in pimientos, Cheddar cheese and butter; heat until melted and crusty.*
- *Add chopped pimientos to mashed potatoes, rice or creamed vegetables.*

Index

For information on how to subscribe to
Ladies' Home Journal, please write to:

Ladies' Home Journal
Box 10895
Des Moines, IA 50336-0895